the UNBELIEVABLE LIFE *of a* COUNTRY BOY

from Country Plowboy to Lt. Col. by Age 30

LT. COL. PETER JACK NEWTON

U. S. Army, Retired

W. Brand Publishing

NASHVILLE, TENNESSEE

j.brand@wbrandpub.com

W. Brand Publishing

www.wbrandpub.com

Cover design by designchik.net

Photography provided by the Newton family

The Unbelievable Life of a Country Boy/Lt. Col. Peter Jack Newton—2nd ed.

Available in Paperback, Kindle, and eBook formats.

Paperback ISBN: 978-1-950385-37-9

eBook ISBN: 978-1-950385-38-6

Library of Congress Control Number: 2020905996

Printed in the United States of America.

CONTENTS

INTRODUCTION

This is the story of the life of Peter Jack Newton, Sr. Not all of it, of course; but some of what he remembers. He will be 90 years old on July 8, 2006 and has just written this in his own handwriting within the past 9 months. Upon completion of the typed manuscript by his daughter Lynn, he began to consider getting it published, just in case someone other than family would be interested. Thus, this book.

We are so very thankful to Almighty God that He has seen fit to bless our dad with good health, mentally and physically, up to this point in his life. However, at the age of 89, the years are beginning to take a toll on him. This book is written according to his memory. It is also written pretty much the way he talks—not always grammatically nor politically correct. It is not guaranteed to be totally factual nor chronological, but he has tried to be as accurate as possible. If there are errors, he would like to apologize and let you know that he did the best he could.

At Daddy's request, the second section of this book is written by us, his children. They are memories from our childhood and recent past. Some of the memories we wrote, we agreed not to publish. Daddy might "tan our hides"! Again, they may not be completely accurate, but they are as we remember them. What a privilege to have had such a wonderful life. We truly thank our parents.

We are so very grateful that our dad is still with us. We still look to him for his guidance, and we still learn from him every day. He is a proud man, and a very thankful man; and we are extremely blessed to be his children. We love him dearly.

Lynn, Ronna, Pete, Pat, and Don
May 2006

Peter Jack Newton Sr.

Jack's father, Robert Lee (Bob) Newton

Jack's mother, Esther V. Newton

CHAPTER 1

I was born July 8, 1916, on the "Family Farm" at Newtonville, South Carolina, in Marlboro County, near Gibson,
North Carolina, which is between Bennettsville, South
Carolina, and Laurinburg, North Carolina. I was born on
Saturday afternoon at four o'clock, with the aid of a black
"Granny Woman" living on the farm. I weighed seven
pounds, nine ounces. My father was Robert Lee Newton
and my mother was Esther Vida Newton. I was named after
my mother's daddy, Peter Smith Newton, my granddaddy. I
was the baby of fourteen–five by my daddy's first wife (four
boys and one girl)–and nine by my mother (five boys and
four girls). The farm has been in the Newton family "since
the Indians left the reservation"–a long time! The farm was
the family's pride and joy–332 acres. It was inherited from
Grandpa Younger Newton, my daddy's daddy.

My father died at the age of fifty-one from pneumonia. I
was four years old, and I had double pneumonia (pneumonia
in both lungs) when he died. Before his death, he directed
my mother to carry me to his funeral–and she did. My Godly
Mother raised us all on that family farm during the depression and "cotton boll weevil days". Cotton was the main
"money crop".

My daddy predicted before his death that within ten years
the farm would be broke and mortgaged for ten thousand dollars–not because of poor management, but because of the boll
weevil and the depression. Those mortgage papers were signed
for ten thousand dollars, ten years to the day from his death, so

I am told. Bad crops from the disastrous boll weevil, and the economy during the depression days, are a matter that no one wished to record or remember. Just about everybody lost just about everything! Land sold for seven dollars ($7.00) per acre, and cotton sold for seven cents ($.07) per pound. The saying was quite often heard, "How in the world can a poor farmer eat? Seven cents cotton and eleven cents meat!"

My uncle had harvested his entire crop one year and had been offered one dollar and twenty-one cents ($1.21) per pound for his "long staple" cotton but was holding it for $1.25 per pound. Well, the stock market on Wall Street busted, the entire economy busted. People committed suicide by jumping from tall buildings in New York as well as many other ways. Farmers lost their farms and homes. Most all of the banks went busted. There was no cash and no credit! Mothers used flowered feed bags (empty chicken feed sacks) to make home-made dresses and shirts for their children. We all went bare-footed—without shoes on—most of the time. We did wear shoes to church, if we had any. My uncle eventually sold his cotton for which he had been offered $1.21 per pound for eleven cents ($.11) per pound. As you very well expected, I suppose, he lost his house and farm anyway—Daddy's wisdom, Mama's fears. Creditors had no mercy. They had no choice. History books are written about all of this—so I'll return to "My Story".

Thanks to the ingenuity of the incredible mothers and homemakers, we existed, but under unbelievable circumstances and conditions. No matter how hard the day, we were in hog heaven at night! We slept under homemade quilts, cotton comforters, on cotton mattresses; or feather mattresses and feather pillows made from plucking the feathers from the geese we raised. If you could not afford the cotton or feather mattresses, you stuffed your mattress cover with straw.

I had plenty of clothes and shoes, hand-me-downs from four brothers. The hand-me-downs were clothes outgrown by older brothers or sisters. They were slightly altered by hand to fit better with the help of an old Singer sewing machine. Quite often, they were adjusted with a safety pin underneath the garment. . .which reminds me of a story of a little boy on the way to school one morning.

He tripped and fell while walking on the beaten path and burst his pants in several places. He was already late because he had worked too long at home before he left for school. He patched up his pants the best that he could with all of the spare safety-pins that he carried "just in case" of an accident. And on to school he went. When he entered the classroom, the teacher greeted him with these words, "Johnny, I see you're a little behind this morning." Whereupon little Johnny answered, "Yes, Ma'am Teacher, but if I had had two more safety-pins, you couldn't (see my behind)!"

I personally had a very similar experience. I was also on my way walking to school one morning, tripped and fell, likewise bursting my pants, but I did not realize it– so on to school I went. Upon arrival, the teacher noticed my split britches; whereupon she advised me of my problem and sent me into the cloak room (a room where you hang your coat, leave your lunch, etc.) to remove my split britches and give them to her. This I did. She took them and sent them to the teacherage for the housekeeper to mend (sew up), leaving my little naked butt in the cloak room until my britches were returned. We won't mention the number of students who had to go to the cloak room for utensils during my extended stay.

You washed the clothes on a metal scrub board in a three-bushel tin tub with water heated by trash and wood fire. If they were real dirty or greasy, or if you had had sickness, you boiled them, the bedding, and bed clothes in an iron pot with homemade lye soap, a product Mama made with Red Devil lye and grease. You hung them on a wire clothesline in the back yard to dry in the sunshine. You ironed (pressed) them with a metal iron, heated in the fireplace (chimney), and put them in a dresser drawer. Many homes did not have closets in that day.

School Time: I started to school and went to church at Boykin, about two miles from home in Newtonville community in Marlboro County, South Carolina. Boykin is near Gibson, North Carolina (two miles). It is about ten miles from Bennettsville, South Carolina. We walked to school, rode a mule, or drove a horse hooked to a buggy. We staked our transportation (horse) out to graze while we were in school. The buggy was full, over-crowded, seated and standing. It was not unusual for one to fall off of the buggy when you made a sharp turn. I fell, or was pushed, more than once. Three teachers—Mrs. Hattie Newton Smith and Mrs. Lucy (Will) Stubbs—had a profound influence on my life; but I guess the third one, Mrs. Theola Brogden was my choice of them all. When school turned out, we rode the mule home, plowed it until dark, and ate supper (we ate breakfast, dinner and supper—not breakfast, lunch, and dinner). You prepared your lessons for tomorrow's school, said your prayers, and went to bed. No TV—not even a radio. The usual prayer was, "Now I lay me down to sleep. I pray the Lord my soul to keep. If I should die before I wake. I pray the Lord my soul to take. Bless Mama, Daddy, all my sisters and brothers. Amen."

We transferred to Robert Fletcher Memorial School near McColl, South Carolina, when the schools consolidated. Fletcher

Memorial, as it was known, was constructed, donated, and dedicated by W. B. and J. A. Fletcher, two well-established and quite successful farmers, in memory of Robert Fletcher who was killed in World War I. It was indeed a beautiful, fantastic, ultra-modern, architectural memorial. There was none other like it around at that time.

Fletcher was about five miles from home. We rode the school bus. We practiced and played football, baseball, and basketball during noon recess and after school in the afternoon. I weighed about one hundred ten pounds. I took pretty much of a beating, but I played the games. I played right field in baseball. Because of my size, I was an excellent batter. I hit the ball as hard as I could swing the bat—with my whole one hundred ten pounds, which knocked the ball hard enough to get it out of the infield, but not hard enough to get it to the outfielder—a "Texas Leaguer"! This gave me a hit almost every time at bat. The ball would usually fall just behind the second baseman and just in front of the right fielder. I had an unbelievable batting average!

I got my five top front teeth knocked out my senior year. A batter knocked a fly ball in almost that exact position described above. Well, I was playing right field, so I was running forward as hard as I could, and the second baseman was running backward as fast as he could, and we collided right under the ball. He was much shorter than I was, so my front teeth sank right into the back of his head. Well, he fell forward and I fell backward, and the ball fell to the ground between us. The game was definitely over for us! He was carried to the hospital, and I was carried to the small-town dentist, who was a "big-time" doctor! Needless to say, I ended up with an upper false teeth plate for the rest of my life. My five top teeth were gone. And I had a terrific bill that I could not pay, and a lifetime to remember it every time I looked in the mirror.

I was considered a well-rounded, well-balanced, rather intellectual student. I was also taught to be polite, respectful, considerate, honest, and dependable. I had lost my father at the age of four, leaving my Godly Mother to teach me, train me, and make me what I had become. She was indeed quite a Lady—poor, but proud. I missed school quite a bit. In the spring, getting the land prepared for planting the crops, and then getting the crops planted. And in the fall, getting the crops harvested. I was an excellent plow boy. I was always chosen to prepare the garden and cultivate the plants. There was very little hoeing left to do if I plowed the plants. You used a hand hoe to remove the weeds and grass that the plow missed.

But I was still quite a competitive student. I was extremely good in math, chemistry, and French. Let's not mention history and geography. I just didn't have time for English with all of the extra time it took for reading. If my mother was poor, but proud, I was surely, little, but loud, and proud!

Jack – High School Senior

We did not consider ourselves poor. We were just average people, but quite successful, established farmers—until the cotton boll weevil came, along with the depression. We were proud of our heritage, and thankful to Almighty God, Our Maker. Church was just as important, or more so, than school. Both were taken seriously. We were taught to be the best we could be, at both.

My proficiency at math and chemistry caused me to be quite popular when the bus arrived at school and before school began. I gave all the answers to homework to those that did not have them. I found out later that I had the highest four-year average of the boys in my class. I might have had the highest average in the entire class had I not been so sharing! However, I would have it no other way until this day. My favorite subject was chemistry.

Let me share a couple of my favorite school projects with you: We had just been taught the horrible effects of sodium and chlorine. In fact, either was quite deadly alone. If you dropped a little stick of sodium in the palm of your hand, it would almost eat through your hand and fall out the back side before you could catch it underneath with the other hand. Likewise, if you breathed chlorine gas into your lungs, it would be almost sudden death. Well, our teacher proceeded to chemically mix the two of them and then evaporate all of the moisture from the crucible, leaving nothing but little salt-like crystals against the sides and in the bottom. He then invited all of us to lick our fingers to moisten them. Then we were to dip them in the crystals and then put them back in our mouth to see how good it tasted. Of course, we all volunteered—HA! yeah, you bet! Whereupon the teacher, getting no volunteers, moistened his finger and rolled it in the crystals, and put it in his mouth! Not just once, but again, and again, and again! We all thought he would drop dead! Well, guess what a surprise he had for us? Remember, either chemical alone would kill you dead, but when chemically combined, they produced plain-old, common table salt! Something that life would not survive without. Can you understand why it got my attention? And it got better, and better. Yes, I am still challenged with chemistry. Before I go further, let me share with you that my greatest ambition was to be a doctor. Remember, I was a farm boy with all of the animals, their sickness, brain, and reproduction, etc. My desire was deep-rooted, and sincere but I had no money.

My favorite memory of my youth was the time we were to catch our own frog and bring it to school with us to "operate" on during our laboratory session. We were to put it to sleep under a laboratory vessel, remove it, cut it open, examine its organs, and put it back to sleep for good; and then to proceed with our classroom hour in the laboratory. What an exciting day it was to be for me. You see, I had planned for days ahead and had selected a prize frog for my special surgery. In addition to my special frog, I had "snitched" (borrowed) a needle and some silk thread from Mama's sewing box to carry along with me to complete my surgery. I wanted to ensure my patient's full recovery. Therefore, I had to have a needle and some thread to sew him back up. Well, the time finally came, preparations were all complete, and we began the procedure. We each successfully got our "patient" to sleep, removed him from the vessel, split him open, examined his organs, made our notes, and proceeded to put him to sleep for good. Well, supposedly. Of course, my surgery went into a little more depth. After I completed my examination and recorded my diagnosis, I secured my needle and thread and proceeded to close the skin (sew him up). After I completed the procedure, I carefully placed him back under the vessel on top of the table;

but instead of closing it down flat on the table, I put a block of wood (which I had previously obtained) under the edge of the vessel to be sure my "patient" did not suffocate, but would have plenty of fresh air while he was in the recovery room. The regular class began, and all was going well, when out of the clear, came this very plain croak. It sounded just like a frog. Then another, and another. Guess what? It WAS a frog! It was MY frog! He had not only survived, he had come out from under the vessel and was hopping along the tabletop. Do you think you can imagine my excitement? How proud I was! Until...all the students, and the teacher, began to stare at my frog. Then came the emergency—one more hop, and he almost went off of the table. Without a thought, or any hesitation, I jumped to my feet, grabbed my frog, and put him in my pocket, and started back to my seat, when the teacher beckoned to me to come to him. He immediately secured the frog and put it safely in a vessel, then proceeded to admonish me for my extracurricular activity. All of which I deserved. I was afraid I was going to get a whipping! But, alas! One of the highlights of my young life, he handed me back my frog and asked me to explain and to show to the class what I had done, the preparation I had made, and the living results of my actions. This I did. He shook my hand and told me to keep up the good work. Then, he kept my frog!

Back to the Farm: I've heard it said many times that "all work and no play would make Jack a dull boy", well, I had my share of both. I personally plowed a mule on my neighbor's farm 14 hours for thirty-five cents ($.35) per day. I was five minutes late hooking the mule to the plow one day after dinner, so my boss docked me a nickel. Five minutes late and he docked my pay five cents! I didn't make but thirty-five cents for fourteen hours. You figure that out. Just figure with me,

I made two and one-half cents per hour. I was docked five cents for being five minutes late, an average of sixty cents for sixty minutes. Remember, I only made two and one-half cents for sixty minutes. He docked me twenty-four times as much as I was making. Highway Robbery! Best I should have gone to jail. . .he should have gone to jail! I have been asked many times what did I do? Quit? I told them, "No, but I wasn't late anymore."

Then to top that off, the boss paid me for a week's work in nickels and dimes. I had a hand full of change. Thirty-five cents per day for six days is two dollars and ten cents, minus the nickel I was docked, left me with two dollars and five cents.

I was a "rich" little boy! But I was also a foolish little boy! I put all of that change in my pocket, and off to school I went Monday morning. During recess, I was wrestling with my little buddies. One of them turned me upside down and every bit of my money fell out of my pocket on the ground without me knowing it. After the school bell rang and I was back in school, I realized all of my money was missing, and I figured I had lost it wrestling. I held my hand up and asked the teacher to be excused to go look for my money. I was refused, because the teacher had made a rule, "No excuse except for the rest rooms." So, I asked to be excused to go to the rest room and was excused. So out I went. Naturally, I was being watched by the teacher. I became even more foolish. I went straight to where I had been playing instead of going to the rest room. Of course, my mind was on my money. Bad news. I didn't find it! More bad news, worse news, when I walked back into the school room, the teacher immediately told me that I had lied to her and sent me straight to the principal's office for my whipping! Woe is me! I had lost all of my money for a whole week's work–two dollars and five cents–and was going to get a whipping, too. When according to me, I had done no wrong until I was forced to because of a teacher who just did not understand. I had lost my pay for eighty-four hours of hard work and had told her the honest truth. I thought the teacher should be punished. I told her that mine were extenuating circumstances. I told her that I had always been taught to tell the truth, and to be honest. This I had done and was being punished for doing so. This got me nowhere. So, to the principal's office I went with my story.

The principal was a huge, tall man. He was about six feet, five inches tall and weighed about two hundred sixty pounds. He taught me agriculture. He was a stern man, but a man of high character. He asked to hear my story. He listened intently. And then he stated his plan. Listen to his conversation (he knows me well, he knew my background, he knew my character). He agreed with me why I did it. He thought the teacher should have understood and made exception to her rule in my case, but I had lied, albeit with good reason. But school rules had to be followed. He had to support his teachers, and appropriate action had to be taken. So, he promptly picked up a paddle, sat a chair in front of me, and told me to reach over the back, bend over, and catch the bottom round of the chair. Whereupon I stood straight up and very firmly (all 90 pounds of me) looked him dead in his eyes and told him he was not going to whip me, because I had worked hard and honest for my money. I had told his teacher the truth, I had been misjudged and mistrusted, and I had taken the only course left available to me. He looked straight at me and told me that he agreed with me. Now for me to listen close and do what he said. Bend over the chair, catch the bottom round, and every time he slapped his thigh with the paddle, lift the chair from the floor, bounce it back down on the floor and holler loud enough for the teacher in the adjoining room to hear me. Then justice would be done, the purpose served, and that all will be well. Well, with somewhat doubting trust and faith, I proceeded to carry out his plan. But when he slapped his thigh with the paddle, I felt it throughout my body, and I fell over the chair! However, after a few moments, I realized all went as planned and we proceeded. Mission accomplished.

I rubbed my eyes until they were red, put on a good pout, re-entered the room, and proceeded to my desk. No questions were asked, and the ordeal was over. However, I still felt that I had sacrificed my character and my integrity.

Well, this young man grew up suddenly and matured quite a bit, or so he thought. He had survived the sports scars and the financial loss and had become quite active in the family farm operations, while still maintaining his high school record grades and popularity.

It was a well-known fact that I did not smoke, drink, or curse. Neither was I a "Sissy". Although I was quite small, and had no daddy, I maintained my self-respect and the respect of my schoolmates. However, those that did smoke wanted me to join their group and cooked up a deal. They all pitched in all of their money—quite a little sum—and offered to give it all to me if I would meet them behind the schoolhouse and smoke a cigarette. They had the cigarette and the matches and would put guards on both corners of the building to be sure I would not be caught. If you were caught smoking, you got a whipping, and you were expelled from school for two weeks. The whipping and being expelled was nothing like what I would get from my Godly Mother when I got home; much less the disrespect that I would feel that I had shown to my mother for her love and training. However, the amount I was offered was more than a month's wages for plowing a mule fourteen hours a day so, I agreed to smoke the cigarette. I had no experience, so I did not know you were supposed to moisten your lips before you placed the cigarette in your mouth. I put it in my lips dry and awaited a light. They struck the match against their trouser leg, and just as they started to put the lighted match to the cigarette, my best buddy reached up and thumped the cigarette from my lips–skin and all! At the very same time, the school principal walked around the corner and said, "Hello boys. You're up to no good. Break it up." My guards were busy watching me instead of the on-coming principal. Paul Harvey's *Rest of the Story*, I've never put a cigarette in my lips since. I have never drunk a drop of whiskey, and the only drugs that I have done was a medicine pill or liquid. Yes, I am now eighty-nine years old, and don't plan to change.

Speaking of whiskey: One experience in my young life had a profound, dynamic effect on my entire life, even until this day. As previously stated, we lived out in the country, ten miles from anywhere, on a dirt country road. When it rained, the road became real muddy with deep ruts in it. So deep that when you turned the wheels, you proceeded to slide right on down it with the wheels sideways until they would suddenly catch and throw you into a 90-degree turn. The main traffic was horse and buggy. Alongside the road was a ditch about two feet wide with sides almost 90 degrees straight up to try to drain the water from the road.

We had a neighbor that lived across the road directly in front of us, and about a half mile back. He would leave home in his buggy and proceed to get drunk. His trusted horse would bring him home just as though he was sober. On this occasion, a terrible cloud came up and it was pouring rain, just thundering and lightening, when he was coming home. I was on the porch at home and saw him coming up the road. When the horse made the 90-degree left turn to go home, the wheels locked and slid down the ruts, until they caught and suddenly made the turn. This threw the drunk man out, and he landed straight up and down the ditch and wedged his big body in the square ditch with his feet upstream, almost like he was in a coffin! This blocked the flowing water in the ditch, and it began to flow over his body, back out into the road. I could see this, and it scared me so bad. Before I thought what I was doing, I was running in the rain to my neighbor in the ditch. I was about ten years old and very small. When I got to him, the water was already overflowing his feet and running over his body.

It was beginning to overflow his chin, mouth, and nose. I was afraid he was going to drown. I pulled on one side of his shoulder, then the other, back and forth, back and forth. I lifted his head and pulled it to the side finally enough to permit the flow of water to go passed his head and proceed down the ditch. This saved his life, I am sure.

My lesson from this: If whiskey could do this to a man, I would never drink a drop. And until this day, I NEVER have. Not in the Army. Not at any party or anniversary. Not anywhere. NOT EVER!

CHAPTER 2

Back to the farm again: We tilled our soil with mules and horses. We broke the land (turned the soil) with a turn plow drawn by two mules, and then prepared it for planting with a disc harrow which chopped the soil into a finer, smoother, texture. We then leveled the land with a drag-tooth harrow, all pulled by a team of two horses (or mules). Then we fertilized the seed bed and planted the seed. After it was up and growing, we cultivated it to keep the weeds and grass out of the crop. We poisoned the growing crop to try to kill the boll weevil and the worms that literally destroyed our crops, but with little success. We used the seed that we had saved from the crops the year before for cotton, corn, grain, etc. We saved our cotton seed at the cotton gin where we carried our harvested cotton to have the seed separated from the lint. The extra seed that we did not need for planting we sold to the ginner, or ground them into cotton seed meal, and used the meal for fertilizer and for animal food. The cotton lint was baled at the gin and sold to cotton mills for processing into clothing and many other products.

We sold our baled cotton for so much per pound to cotton buyers or the ginning merchant. Cotton was our main source of income. The money went back to the merchant usually, but not necessarily, to pay our debts for various products such as food, clothing, fertilizer, etc. The store was called a General Merchandising store. They carried almost anything you wanted or needed. We did not have enough money to supply our needs so we were credited at the store until we could harvest our crops. Our crops and homes were mortgaged to secure this credit. If you couldn't pay your debts, you could lose your farm and home. You were at the mercy of the lender (usually the merchant or the bank). If you did not pay your debt and the lender let you slide (carry your debt over another year), the interest on the loan was usually exorbitant. It made the debt even harder to repay. So, you sacrificed more and more until you were able to pay off the debt or lose all you possessed. This procedure was called foreclosure. As I have previously said, many, many lost everything they possessed. It was truly a Great Depression.

Corn was much easier to grow and harvest than cotton. It was used for family food–grits, hominy, meal, etc. You could have yellow or white. It depended on the variety you planted. Cornbread–yellow or white–was as much a staple as was flour, which was made from wheat, and used to make biscuits, dumplings (pastry), cakes, etc. The other main use for corn was to feed the livestock. It was their major food. It was fed by the ear–the corn was still on the cob–to horses and hogs. It was shelled (removed from the cob) and fed, whole grain or ground, to chickens, turkeys, small pigs, etc. It could also be cracked for small chicks, turkeys, etc.

The ear of corn was harvested by hand–pulled from the stalk by hand–thrown into a wagon which was pulled by two mules and hauled to the barn (corn crib). It was thrown by hand from the wagon into the corn crib and stored for future use.

When used for family food, the corn was shucked in the barn where it was stored, usually on cold, and/or rainy days. To shuck it, you pulled the shucks down the ear by hand and broke them off at the butt of the ear. Then you shelled it–removed the corn from the cob by a hand sheller–a gadget with a big wheel and a long handle to turn it with—or shelled it by hand. You threw the corn cob (what the grains of corn were attached to) away; or you could use it for starting fires. You then take the corn to a grist mill, where it is ground—course for hominy, finer for grits, and very fine for meal. You pay for the grinding service by toll—a specified amount of the corn. The huge grinding wheel (rock) is turned by water. Corn is also harvested for Roasting Ears, (formal terminology for what we called Roas'neers) which you prepare by boiling on-the-cob in a pot of water on the stove; or it may be stewed, canned, or frozen for eating.

Grain is also grown for livestock, poultry, and family food. Wheat, for instance, is now harvested by a machine called a reap and binder, or combine. It is then carried to a flour mill and ground into flour. Grain, in its growing stage, can also be used for grazing cattle. Watermelons, cantaloupes, cucumbers, and other products are also grown. Tobacco is also a big money crop for many; but you have to have a government allotment to grow it. Soya beans (soybeans) are also a very good money crop and easy and cheap to produce and harvest. They are also legumes. They produce nitrogen nodules on their roots and store the nitrogen in the soil. Soybeans have many uses, even cooking oil.

I must come back to cotton and its production. It requires much labor and expense to produce. Some aspects of the production require labor and expense throughout the entire year. You save the seed to plant from the previous crop. You have them cleaned and treated for diseases of the plant and in the soil, and some insects and mites. You treat them with a chemical to give the young plants a healthy start. It may well determine if you produce a profitable harvest or go into debt. One big factor in cotton's favor is its tolerance for unfavorable weather conditions. Droughts or excessive rains may reduce its production and the quality of the harvest, but seldom is there a total loss–or a real disaster.

You must fight insects and diseases from cotton's young stages of growth to maturity. The chemicals and applications are very expensive and dangerous. You must also stay on the job controlling the weeds and grass throughout the growing season, or they will cause a total loss.

The cotton plant produces little squares that grow into blossoms. The blossoms produce bolls, and the bolls open, producing the white cotton locks, which is the lint and seeds that you harvest and market for your profit–you hope. If all goes well, a good yield is a bale to the acre. The higher the yield, the greater the profit. It takes about a bale to the acre to break even. All over a bale to the acre is jubilation.

The culprit, the thief, the insect that usually causes a crop failure is the boll weevil. It lays its egg in the above mentioned square or blossom, and it develops into a little grub (worm) which devours the fruit of the cotton plant and emerges from the destroyed square a full-grown boll weevil. The cycle completed, the new boll weevil begins a new generation, and continues to carry on to full destruction! So, instead of the bale per acre, the devastating and uncontrollable boll weevil had cut our production to one fourth to one half bale per acre, or less. Our losses became greater and greater. Our debts became greater and greater. The depression was getting greater and greater. All of this at a very critical stage in my life. I was about to graduate from high school. What should I do? What could I do? The family farm, my aging mother, our very existence! What would my daddy have done? His prediction before his death was about to become a reality—the farm would be broke and mortgaged for ten thousand dollars ten years after his death.

It was quite obvious at the time, with the terrible depression, that there would be no further education and no employment after graduation from high school. In fact, your very existence was somewhat questionable. So, with all the children gone by now but me and my dear mother with the indebted farm, it was quite evident to this young lad that he and the Good Lord had quite a task in front of them. I did have some help already, however. My deceased daddy had somehow legally, before his death, with the aid of business friends and legal counseling, and his smart intellectual expertise, (and I understand that was just a partial description of his ingenuity and accomplishments) had devised some legal maneuvering whereby the farm could not be lost before his youngest child—that was me—became twenty-one.

In the meantime, my precious mother was not too dumb either. By this time, the farm and home had some nine mortgages and judgments against it. And with the falling value of farmland, and the lack of finances, it had become impossible to get, or devise, any way, or plan, to save the farm—or so it seemed—from mortgage foreclosures. Well, think again!

This country girl, with a fourth grade education, nine children, and the step-children, no husband, and no money, manipulated a deal with the help of a most wonderful business man—an insurance salesman—to sell the virgin timber (that is timber that has never been cut or harvested), and use the money from the timber sale from the mortgaged land to pay off the first mortgage on the land and home. This sale could be legally possible only if the money from the timber from the land was used to pay off the first mortgage on the farm and home. They followed this procedure, and thereby giving my Godly Mother the first mortgage on the estate.

You must hear the rest of the story—the land that had been appraised (valued) at seven hundred dollars per acre in the best of times—at the peak of its value—was now practically worthless because there was no one who had money to buy it. The value of the first mortgage in cash was more than the entire farm was worth. To state it plain and simple—if the other creditors—mortgage holders—joined together and had the land auctioned and sold, then Mama would get the entire farm, debt free, because it would take the entire proceeds to pay off her first mortgage. Therefore, the farm stayed intact, until the youngest child (that was me), according to Daddy's will, became twenty-one.

So, we retained the farm and continued to sharecrop it with good old "colored" families. To sharecrop with others, the landowner furnished the land, mules and horses to cultivate it, fertilizers, seeds, and all necessary expenses but the labor, and got two-thirds of the crop. The tenant (share-cropper) furnished all the labor to produce the crop and got one-third of the harvest. The landowner furnishes the tenant all of his needs—food, house, clothing, doctor bills, drugs, etc. He recovers his advanced loan when they sell the crops, and the tenant gets his one-third of the sale. If the crops do not bring enough to pay the tenant's debts, the landlord bears the loss. If the agreement and conditions are satisfactory and pleasing to both parties—the landlord and the tenant—they may farm together for life, and even for generations. They become almost as family and become very, very fond of each other. These mutual benefits are good for both parties.

On one occasion during the flu (influenza) epidemic, one of our long-time tenants—a man and his wife—were helping

Mama with her sick children day and night–cooking for them, feeding them, sleeping with them, and bathing them–whatever became necessary around the house, and feeding and tending to the farm livestock and barn work, when the man got sick. We all thanked God that by this time some of the children were well enough to go to his home, stay with him, and care for him until–you guessed it–the woman got sick also. We combined all of our resources. Everybody doctored and fed everybody. We were all really in one accord–or predicament! Thanks to Almighty God, we all survived. They were really one of us until death parted us years later. There was no slavery, no cruelty–just business all the time. Everybody trusted everybody. Everybody helped everybody. People shared with each other. Noone locked their doors at night, or when they left home. Families doctored and cared for other families when they were sick and helped dig their grave when they died.

PETER JACK NEWTON

CHAPTER 3

Churches had revivals, big meetings, under huge tents with dynamic preachers, evangelists, spirit-filled singing, altar calls, shouting, and praying that would blot out your sins, lift you right out of your seat, and right into heaven's door! The saved would minister person-to-person, one-on-one, to the lost and youth from bench-to-bench under the tents, or pew-to-pew in the church. If storms came up and lights went out, the preaching, singing, and praying kept right on. The services were usually held in late summer or early fall to best fit into the farming operations when the least labor was needed.

The huge tents would have wooden benches on top of saw dust that had been spread on the ground, with aisles open down to the pulpit. "Cyclone Mack" McClendon was our evangelist on several occasions. He was quite a character. He opened his message one evening with the exclamation, "God Damn! It's hot in here!" Then proceeded to point his finger at a man in the pew and said, "That is what I heard you say as I passed down the aisle." On another occasion, the people were all assembled and waiting, but no Cyclone Mack or so they thought! Cyclone Mack was never late. Precisely on the hour of worship, this voice came out from behind the pulpit. As you looked closer you saw this long finger sticking up over the pulpit pointing upward toward heaven and the voice saying, "I am the Lord thy God; He that believeth in me, though he were dead, yet shall he live." Then you see the body of Cyclone Mack as he rises slowly to full stature behind the pulpit.

On another occasion, Preacher Harvey Danner was our evangelist. His favorite was to plead with you that instead of cursing–taking God's name in vain, such as "God Damn It"–say "God Danner" and I'll pray for you. Mama loved Preacher Danner. He was soft-spoken and had a wonderful personality. She said he was so good with, and for, the children. She named her second child Harvey after Preacher Danner.

Esther, Bob & children
Jack (about a yr. old) on his mother's lap

One of my mother's favorite stories about the tent meeting revivals was shared many times. Daddy had died, and Mama had the older boys to hook the horse to the buggy for the trip to the tent revival as usual. Of course, the buggy was full of Newtons–large and small. In fact, so full that if one was missing you would never notice. Now for Paul Harvey's *The Rest of the Story*: Mama had her baby (me) at the tent meeting on her lap sleeping, when all of a sudden, she felt the urge to shout (praise the Lord) and testify all over the place! So, something had to be done with the baby; the baby had to go. So, under the wooden bench, on the saw dust, I was placed—sound asleep. Well, as Mama shouted, praising The Lord, the services ended, Mama loaded her brood (crew) on and in the buggy, full of joy and thanksgiving, and home they went. When they got home and unloaded—you guessed it—Mama missed her baby boy. So, off to the tent they sped, worried to death about the baby awakening alone—in the dark! What would I do? Where would I be? Mama praying, "Good Lord, take care of my baby!" Well, what do you think? You're right—I was still there, right where Mama placed me, under the bench, in the saw dust, sound asleep. Now you know, the rest of the story.

I learned to sleep in church at an early age. And guess what? I've gotten better at it as I've grown older. Even through my eighty-ninth birthday. I am truly a professional now. I can sleep sitting straight up in the pew—never drop my head or change my position!

I've got a new one going now—I have two hearing aids—one in each ear. When I want to get the preacher's attention, or when I see him glance at me, I'll be adjusting my hearing aids. He doesn't know if I'm turning him on or turning him off! Well, as I got older, I got better—at deception, that is. When my older brother would go out courting (dating), he would take me with him to get me out of Mama's way, knowing that I would be asleep, all tucked in, on the back seat by the time he got to his girlfriend's house. Well, are you ready for the rest of the story? You've got that right! I was seldom asleep—then or later. I would play possum, play sound asleep—dead to the world—and watch and listen. Boy, did I learn fast! No student in any school was smarter or learned faster or remembered better. My brother was a Casanova—a lover boy. He was quite a ladies' man! All the girls loved him.

But you ain't heard nothing yet. Just imagine, a farm boy, nature lover with a natural curiosity, and a professional teacher (my brother). What did I grow up to be? Let your imagination be your answer–I'll survive.

When I was a young lad, the girls would pick me up, hold me in their arms, hug and kiss me, and say, "You look just like your brother." But, as I grew older, what I got was, "You look and act just like your brother!" Well, I should have! All of those lessons were not forgotten, they were put into practice. I'm sure if I had been graded, I would have gotten an A+ on the course. The plus was for my personal extra-curricular activities.

With this background, a senior in high school, the terrible economic conditions and the farm situation like it was, I made quite an estimate of the situation. I was beginning to think quite seriously about my future. I requested a business conference with my mother. After all, I was all of sixteen years old, and the male head of the household. But this was not all of my attributes. Most of all, I was madly in love with the prettiest, cutest, sweetest young lady in the whole school. It was even more than that. She was the prettiest girl I had ever seen! And even more, she was the heroine in the senior class play. Guess what? I was the hero! In fact, she had written the quotation under my senior picture in the high school annual, "As to his women, though he may taunt and flaunt them, he may live with but will never live without them." She liked that one better than the one she did the year before, "Peter Jack Newton–the cream of the crop–when you get him started–he is hard to stop!" To top it all off, in the senior class play, in the final scene, I propose to her; and as the stage curtain is falling, she looks up in my eyes and accepts my proposal. That was supposed to be the grand finale. But it didn't end up quite that way. Before the curtain completely closed, the hero places a kiss on the lips of his beautiful heroine. This was not permitted in those olden days, but the entire audience came to their feet, clapping their full approval!

I think that is all that saved my hide.

At this time, my main concern in life was to continue to take care of my mother and provide a home and a future for my future bride.

With all of this on my mind, I faced my mother at the business conference, which she had granted. I confronted her with my master plan or proposition. I would be her overseer, farm operator, farm manager—whatever—if she would provide the home, share her home, with me and my future bride.

To start with: #1. She would give me four chickens—three hens and one rooster. That would provide me and my bride with two eggs for breakfast, and one a day to save for setting when one of the hens decided to become a mother. The rooster would fertilize the egg by mating with the hen. The hen would quit laying. (The hens usually lay one egg per day.) We would set the hen on fifteen eggs. She would set on them fourteen days. The breast heat and feathers would incubate the eggs. They would hatch out all together. The baby chicks would develop inside the eggshell like a baby develops inside the mother's womb. If the mother hen was prevented from returning to her nest of eggs for some reason for too long a time when she came off of the nest once a day for food and water, the eggs would get cold and the little baby chick would die inside the shell. If all went well, the fully developed baby chick would use its little beak to peck the shell open and burst its way out. They would remain in the nest for about twenty-four to thirty-six hours. The mother hen would bring them off of the nest and work diligently trying to provide her baby chicks with food and water. She would scratch the soil and piles of debris for bugs and worms, stopping periodically to hover the little chicks under her wings and breast feathers to keep them warm. At night, the little ones would stay tucked under the mother hen from sundown (almost dark) until daylight. The rooster would crow to announce the breaking of dawn (early daylight).

Of course, the mother hen with so many babies needed help to feed and nurture them. We would feed the chicks, and the mother, cracked corn (tiny bits when babies–larger pieces later) and then the whole grain. As they developed into grown chickens, the females (hens) would be kept to lay eggs and reproduce and eventually follow the above procedure. The males (roosters) would be killed as fryers while they were young and developing (three to five pounds) or when mature for baking, roasting, chicken and dumplings, etc.

#2. In addition to the three hens and one rooster, Mama must give me a female hog (sow). I could breed the female to Mama's male hog (boar), and in about ninety days we would have a litter of little pigs–usually five to fourteen– about seven to nine average. Again, the females could be kept to reproduce as needed and the males for slaughter when mature. Any females not kept for breeding stock were also slaughtered at about 220-500 pounds.

Requirement #3: For my expert services, Mama was to give me a milk cow (female). Again, I could breed my female cow to Mama's male cow (bull), and in about nine months, we would have a little baby calf. And again, the female calf could be kept to continue reproduction, or be slaughtered along with the little bulls as needed for beef or sold at the market when they weighed about 400-700 pounds. The mother cow, of course, provided milk, cream, and butter for the families.

Final requirement #4: I was to receive ten percent (10%) of the net profit from the farm production. This would supply, hopefully, items that we could not produce on the farm, such as doctor bills, drug bills, clothing, shoes, coffee, sugar, and of course, baby diapers for the little one, if one came along! And money for the church.

If you have not yet figured out the method in my madness to provide for my household, I will sum it up for you: If things go as planned and itemized above, the results should be:

The chickens would provide (1) fried eggs for breakfast (2) boiled eggs and deviled eggs for dinner and supper (3) eggs for pancakes, salads, cakes, cookies, pies, etc. (4) colored eggs for Easter (5) fried chicken (6) chicken and rice (7) baked chicken (8) chicken and dumplings (9) chicken pastry and (10) chicken salad for dinner and supper, picnics, church affairs, and especially when company comes. We must not forget hot chicken broth and chicken soup for the sick and the cold weather.

The hogs would provide (1) country ham with redeye gravy (2) sausage to go with grits we have made from ground corn from the farm and the fried eggs provided by the chickens to help make our breakfast (3) for variety, we will use cured bacon in lieu of the ham or sausage (4) we still have the spare ribs to serve (5) the ham hock to season with (6) pork chops (7) and of course, we cannot forget the ever popular bar-b-que for cookouts or sandwiches.

The cow would provide (1) milk for the morning breakfast drink (2) milk for the cereal (3) cream for the coffee (4) butter for the toast and grits (that is, if you prefer butter to red-eye gravy) (5) butter for baking (6) rib-eye steak (7) prime rib (8) sirloin (9) round steak (10) cubed steak (11) hamburger (12) stew beef and rice.

Now, if you will do me a favor–prepare your menu for me for breakfast, dinner, and supper (or breakfast, lunch, and dinner), and I will give you mine.

How about breakfast: Country ham, fried eggs, grits with red-eye gravy, buttered toast, coffee and cream, (or substitute country sausage or bacon for the ham), and fresh sweet milk to drink.

Now for dinner, lunch, or supper: Fried chicken, baked chicken, chicken and dumplings, chicken salad–your choice– with side order and dessert.

Or: Fried country ham with rice and red-eye gravy–or your choice of pork chop or bar-b-que–with side order and dessert.

Or: Prime rib, rib-eye steak, sirloin steak, hamburger, or stew beef and rice–with side order and dessert.

Then for snacks and goodies, when and if desired: home-made ice cream, milkshakes, cakes, pies, cookies, etc.

Now grade me on my plans to provide for my household. How would you like to eat with me?

One more question: If reproduction increased normally, as would be expected, with the chickens, hogs, and cows, what would be my status in ten years? You don't have to mention the five or six children.

CHAPTER 4

Well, my mother was seriously considering the business proposition, when suddenly one day my whole life was to be changed. A gentleman from Bennettsville drove into our yard, introduced himself, and told me that he had been told by my neighbors that I was the best driver in the county. They said I had been driving since I was seven years old. The declaration came about because there wasn't room for me in the car except on the driver's lap! Remember, at this time, there were ten of us–the nine children and Mama. So, as I sat in the driver's lap, I learned how to steer the car, change the gears, slow down, speed up, start and stop the car, be alert, yield the right of way, and judge distance and speed, etc. There was no driver's license required at that time, so I had been driving since I could see over the steering wheel. I had never had an accident. I didn't drink. I was courteous, and respected the other driver. So, I guess I wasn't too bad!

So, what did this have to do with the visitor? He was going to Wofford College in Spartanburg, South Carolina, to carry his son. His son could drive up to the college, but the visitor didn't particularly like to drive, so he wanted me to drive him back home. I had always wanted to see Wofford College since my oldest half-brother had gone there. Now here was my chance! My brother was quite brilliant. He was so young when he completed high school that they did not admit him into Wofford but sent him to Carlisle Fitting School for one year. It was like a junior college for Wofford. He went to Wofford the second year and graduated with all kinds of honors–still in knee pants. What a reputation!

We made all of the arrangements for the trip. I told him I would be glad to go and drive for him, and Mother approved.

I started brown bagging. My Mother packed my clothes (one pair of underwear, one handkerchief, and one pair of socks) in a brown paper bag. And one dollar and twenty-five cents in my pocket. I haven't figured the socks out yet.

While waiting with the gentleman at Wofford for his son to matriculate (I thought you did that out behind the barn), I saw these rich boys (rich men's sons) coming in and talking about going downtown to get a part-time job–I thought to help pay their way through college. I found out later it was to have extra money that Dad and Mom didn't know about to spend promiscuously. So, out I go behind them to see if I could get a job, too.

The first place they go into is a grocery store. As I approached the store, they came out of the store just laughing. I thought they had gotten a job, so in I went to try my hand. The first question I got asked was, "Why do you think I would hire you?" My answer was, "To get money for my education. I am trying to work my way through school." His reply, "Didn't you know I just threw those three guys in front of you out of my store?" My answer was, "I am not with those guys. I am on my own." He seemed surprised, asked me a few more questions, and hired me to work afternoons and Saturdays. This causes me to send the gentleman that I was to drive home for, home alone. This, I apologized for with all of my heart. I had broken my promise, but the gentleman understood and was real proud that he had helped me get to Wofford.

Now I find myself alone, away from home, with my brown bag and one dollar and twenty-five cents in my pocket. I immediately sign up for R.O.T.C. (Reserve Officers Training Corps) to get army clothes to wear. You had to wear the uniform three days a week to drill and to class. You got that right—I wore them six days a week. And what did I do for food and lodging? I signed up with the Infirmary Matron to be her assistant for room and sleep. Food to eat would have to come later.

Now, how did I get to sign up for college? The college treasurer just happened to be my oldest brother's roommate at Wofford many years ago! I chatted with him about my ambitious problem of working my way through college. He was quite a man. He immediately got my high school records and found out that I had the highest high school academic average for boys. That gave me a free scholarship. Now, I find myself in college. Even if it was several days later—which, of course, I had to make up in my spare time. I also signed in as a Ministerial student, which gave me free tuition, since Wofford College is a Methodist institution.

Well, I still needed at least a little pocket change. So, I got a job as usher at the State Theatre at night. Then contacts enabled me to also get a job representing a local jeweler, selling jewelry on the side. Other contacts caused me to go see a lovely lady who ran a boarding house in town who needed a house boy—someone to serve breakfast at dawn and supper at dark. You're right again—I became her boy for my meals.

By now, believe it or not, I'm doing more working than I am studying or sleeping. But with everybody's help and sympathy, I finished my freshman year. I had taken a full course. Guess what? I passed all of my subjects! But I was somewhat in debt to the college.

Here we go into summer but before I left college, I secured all of my jobs except the boarding house waiter. In addition, however—too tempting to miss—I secured the job of representing a dry-cleaning firm, a laundry firm, and a shoe repair shop. (Much more about the laundry job later.) Plus, a BIG plus, Mama Bear—Carlisle Hall Matron—honored me with a fulltime waiter's job in the mess hall, and free room in one of her spare rooms in her apartment. Except for my bout with the mumps, this ended my experience in the infirmary. What a blessing! A whole new lease on life. This new development guaranteed me free room and board to add to my free tuition. I had helped Mama Bear as substitute waiter any time one of her regular waiters was out.

Where, and how, do you think I spent the summer? With Mother at home? No! Off to Myrtle Beach I go thumbing (hitch-hiking). I get a job at Ye Olde Tavern, the classiest joint on the beach front. I barter to furnish all the cash to pay at the counter for all I serve in the lounge or on the deck out over the breakers. Then I would collect all of the bills from the customers. If I don't collect, I lose. O.K. But the rest of my deal was, any extra I make, I keep. Ahh! But what a deal. I not only got my money back, plus the tips, I got all of the double, triple, and quadruple payments. Those extra payments came about when couples or parties of any number would each, trying to be nice, pay the entire bill at the table—and leave, arguing about who was going to pay. (Being half drunk meant more than being nice). So, I reaped the benefits! This deal the owners bought because it helped them not to lose what some customers would order and then in the busy moments leave without paying. My country personality and courtesy, as well as being on the job, paid big dividends.

The Tavern was owned by a Greek and his beautiful wife. I ate at the restaurant and slept under the deck with the waves breaking and rushing up on my feet at high tide, until the pretty lady felt sorry for me and gave me a bed in the establishment.

Now, I've got it made! So much for the rest of the summer. It was quite a success financially for this farm boy.

Back to college for my sophomore year. (They tell me sophomore means wise fool.) I hitch-hiked back to school—nothing new—I hitch-hiked everywhere I went. I arrived a few days early to establish all of my contacts and secure my jobs. All starts well. I sign up for college and start all of my classes with all of the other students. I have a little more pocket change, which now has become spending money, and more clothes. One Saturday, I take off from the grocery store to go get my sister, Ada, into a football game free (Wofford was playing Clemson, and they would beat Clemson 14-13) and I get my pay docked and warning of loss of my job. Well, it would have cost me more to pay her way into the game than I would have made all day at the store. I was fired later anyway.

My Spanish professor—Dr. Salmon—had learned of my determination to go to college, and rather than see me flunk, moved me from alphabetical order seating to the front row, center, so as to step on my toes when walking back and forth to wake me up and keep my attention. (I had Spanish first period after dinner.) Then his pretty Spanish wife had me over to their house the night before the Spanish exam to brief me to be sure I passed.

My sincerity, my courtesy, and my attitude served me well, and paid big dividends on all my jobs. I almost had more than I could handle but my buddies would help me take up and deliver the dry cleaning, laundry, and shoe repair. It was so rewarding it was almost fun. My confidence and my pride grew as my business and friendships developed. I worked and went to school my first two years about twenty hours of the twenty-four hour days. That left four hours to sleep and study (plus what I slept in class).

So comes to a close my sophomore year. I had passed all of my courses and paid all of my bills. But before I leave college for the summer, I improve my business status. I would continue to wait tables in the mess hall, (now Mama Bear's Special Baby Boy) and continue to represent my dry cleaning firm, my shoe repair shop, my laundry business, and my jeweler; and would be in advanced R.O.T.C., for which I would draw some pay.

I had also been hired to represent several other dry-cleaning businesses. From this deal, I subcontracted each company to another student for one-half my profit. You might say I had a monopoly on the business. I gave up my job as usher in the State Theatre, and as I've stated already, I was fired from the grocery store, because I refused to weigh my thumb when I used the scales. This meant that when you placed the product–cheese, etc.–on the scales, you would drop your thumb on the platform to make the product weigh more; thereby increasing the profit for the store. Getting fired hurt my feelings but increased my pride. With a fresh determination and ambition, I took off my apron, threw it at the manager, and out the door I went, headed downtown, quite confident, to better my status in life.

I passed up the Elite, a classy drug store and college hangout, and went into S. H. Kress 5 & 10 cent store but found the manager was out. My choice was S. H. Kress 5 & 10 cent store because all the pretty girls worked there. So, I pondered a while–a short while–and to McClellan's 5 & 10 cent store I went, just a few doors down the street. Straight up the stairs I went to the manager's office–unannounced–where I found two men. I knocked, was invited in, and was told to state my business. I asked if one of the men was the manager, and the one who invited me in confirmed his position. I proceeded to introduce myself and state my business—I was working my way through college and wanted a job. He asked me to state my case—whereupon I told him I had just been fired and why, and that my objective was to better myself, and if he needed a man, he would not find a better one. He asked me about my personal habits. I told him I had never smoked a cigarette, had never drunk a drop of whiskey, and I did not have time to play. So, he asked me what I did with my spare time. I then gave him the details—to which he responded, "You don't have any time left to work." To which I answered, "If I could get a job as stock boy helper, I could hire student helpers with my college jobs, but I would have to keep my job in the mess hall as waiter. Then he asked me if this was the first place I had asked for a job. I answered, "No, Sir. I stopped at Kress's first." His response was, "Why didn't the Kress manager hire you?" to which I responded, "He wasn't in." Thereupon, he told me he was going to hire me. But the man sitting with him said, "You can't do that! I have already hired him. He came to my place first." You get the story, the "other man" was the manager of Kress. So, after some discussion, the Kress manager convinced the McClellan manager that he needed me worse, and that he was taking me back to his store (Kress) and putting me to work at (looking at his watch) three o'clock. I told him I would be there tomorrow and thanked them both profusely.

But now for more of the story: He was putting me to work right now, to which I replied, "Sir! It is already twenty minutes after three." To which he replied, "Oh! But you came in my store at 3 o'clock!" So, I became a S. H. Kress "stock boy" at 3 o'clock on a beautiful Friday afternoon. And I remained a TRUE, dedicated, enthusiastic, ambitious, and very proud

S. H. Kress part-time employee. This has remained one of the big highlights of my entire life.

Mr. Gardner–the Kress manager was my boss, yes, and, I, his pride and joy! He constantly taught me, "all he knew" and "I taught him more." No young boy who lost his dad at four years old, the baby of fourteen, living (surviving) on a farm, could be more fortunate. God really sent me an angel. Mr. Gardner made me his personal admiration society, his example for others, his head stock boy. He made me manager of the Sweets (candy) department. He said that included the "Pretty Young Ladies Club" but, it was against company rules to fraternize with the girls. Of course, that did not bother me, even when I was downstairs in the candy stockroom, or upstairs in the dark aisles of the general store stockroom with my favorites–ALONE.

One incident, I recall–it just happens to come to mind. I was upstairs in the stockroom with one of the prettiest, cutest, sweetest girls of them all, of course, minding my own business in the dark, when I heard Mr. Gardner coming up the steps–whistling–not because he was happy, but to warn me he was coming. Of course, he did not want to catch me fraternizing with the female employees–store rules! He would have to fire me. I did not want him to catch me, so I took off running down the aisle in the dark, and ran right into a six-foot rolling shelf-truck (the vehicle you use to send merchandise downstairs on the elevator to the sales counters) and broke my nose. Of course, Mr. Gardner knew what was going on so (he told me, in private, later) he just happened to remember something he forgot downstairs and turned around and went back downstairs and saved my hide.

One other incident–much more sickening: I had worked all of my first week in the candy supply room–downstairs alone—with access to every kind of candy in a 5 & 10 cent store—and you know I did? I had sampled every kind of candy in the supply room—really sampled in excess. At closing Saturday night, Mr. Gardner invited us all to the ice cream bar for refreshments—and he served the ice cream. When he came to me, he complimented me and welcomed me to the clan, and dipped me extra helpings. Remember, I'm already so full of candy I'm sick to the stomach—so the more he dipped, the sicker I got. You guessed it again, I fessed up, which was no surprise to him. He informed me that he had served my portion in a special dish so he could divide mine among the others, because he knew that I wouldn't be eating any ice cream tonight. After a big laugh, we all—they all—finished their ice cream and cookies, and we all went home. Home was about two miles from the store to the college dormitory (Carlisle Hall—the dorm where all of the poor boys stayed). I walked, mostly ran, down the railroad track (short cut) back and forth to work and to classes.

That brings up another story that probably should not be told. It would take me about a half-hour to walk from school to work. As Mr. Gardner would tell you, when class was over at the end of an hour, Mr. Gardner would punch me in on the hour on the time clock at the store. He said it made timekeeping and bookkeeping easier and simpler. Of course, you know what it meant to me. He justified the procedure by saying that I was walking on his time.

One other fun time: For your information, I did not have the money at the time to pay to go to the Wofford-Clemson football game, so I scaled the fence. But when I hit the ground on the inside of the stadium, the official blew the whistle for me; and it scared me so bad that I ran back out of the gate, instead of running over and getting lost in the crowd (my sophomore year—remember wise fool). Needless to say,

I devised other means. (No stupid fool, HA!) Well, by now I'm back at school for my junior year. And I must admit, quite a different character. Prouder than ever, more experienced than ever, better trained than ever, and more confident than ever–in fact, I guess ALMOST cocky–at least, more professional and more mature. I was one of "The Best", and everybody made me feel that I was.

I picked up where I left off at the end of my sophomore year. I felt as though I almost had it made. I was even with the school–almost–with my expenses; and I began to enjoy some social life. I was in advanced R.O.T.C. and was asked to join the National Guard–which I did–for a little extra money. But what a surprise I was to get! Our National Guard unit was called to active duty and sent to Pennsylvania on Strike Duty. I subcontracted all of my jobs that I could and was put on leave status with Kress.

This was certainly a new experience for me. I found it very difficult to threaten my fellow man with a loaded rifle, much less a fixed bayonet. But I survived. I returned to school, resumed command of all my jobs, resumed my social activities and started some new ones. But they had to be limited due to all my other activities necessary to stay in school.

By now I was well known, and well received in the business world of Spartanburg–due largely to Mr. Gardner, Manager of Kress. I also was much better known and well-received by the Wofford College social circles, and the Converse College ladies. When I ever got to go out socially, it was usually with a different young lady from different groups involved by invitation. It seemed to have been assumed that I could not be had by any one girl. And I couldn't. Time from business duties would not permit. But, Wow! What a reputation! And it did not take me too long to cultivate that train of thought. What a time this poor country boy was having!

I eventually met possibly the most outstanding young lady in Spartanburg–not only socially, but in many other ways. Her dad owned a lot of the city, including a laundry I represented and referred to above, but I did not know it at the time. Each member of the family had their own car, and I had none. What an added attraction. The young lady became very special. She would take me to work and bring me back to college, if possible, especially if I needed it. Her personal car soon became available for my needs. I took a job with a very, very prominent lawyer and top politician, delivering legal papers and summons for him for so much a paper and so much a mile. You are right again–my lady friend's car became quite an asset used without question. Even to the extreme: Guy Lombardo and his famous Royal Canadians were playing at a dance in Charlotte on a Saturday night, and she could not get off, so to Charlotte I went in her car–alone! I'll tell no further secrets. I took a friend (my sister's roommate in Charlotte) to the dance. I'll never clear my conscience but I was beginning to be and act like a college boy. Back from the ridiculous to the sublime. My girlfriend and I became very, very close, and remained so until the middle of my senior year. I had assumed we would be married, until one night I had made an engagement, and lo and behold, she informs me of something she had heard, so she would not be taking me. And without her I wouldn't be going anyway–so, I wouldn't be going. Wow! What a challenge! And what a mistake! What she had told me she had heard was absolutely untrue. But nevertheless, the challenge–more than that–the threat. It hurt me deeper, deeper, and still deeper. Until the sad response. I picked up the phone and called a very good friend's sister and told her if she could get her brother's car, we could go to my engagement together. She did get the car, and we did go.

What a tragedy! That was the last of my dream for any further relations with my very dear friend—my future bride.

CHAPTER 5

I have gone from the middle of my junior year to the middle of my senior year. I have skipped summer camp for R.O.T.C. students, a trip to the west coast, and the starting of a new business. Let's start with R.O.T.C. summer camp. It was held at Fort McClellan, Alabama. It was quite an experience. We learned a lot about the army, especially its "Plans and Training" program, and its discipline. But probably, most of all, the leadership of its Officers. What a challenge! What an incentive!

It is now 1936 with something new—something BIG! The World's Fair in California! I'm in Alabama, a long way from South Carolina, but still a long way to California. What a thought of attending for a farm boy to have. It was decision time. I count my money and start hitch-hiking to California having made the following decision: When one-half of my money is gone, no matter where I am, I change directions, and head for South Carolina. Remember back in those days, times were entirely different. As I have said before, no one locked their doors at night, or when they left home. Robbery or murder, or kidnapping was something you even seldom read about. There was no fear, really.

I have made up my mind, and I am on my way. I have gotten from camp to the outskirts of Montgomery on the highway to The World's Fair. I am neat. I am clean. I am alert. I have a smile on my face, and as the new cars come by, I have a thumb in the air. When the older cars are passing, I casually have my back turned. I have hardly gotten poised, with my charm turned on, when a brand new Airflow Chrysler pulls up beside me and asks where I am going. My confident answer was, "To the World's Fair in California." They responded, "Hop in. We're on our way to Phoenix, Arizona." Of course, I thought this was a joke, but it was for real! They were from Gastonia, North Carolina, close to Charlotte. It was a man and his wife, and their twelve-year-old boy. They were the owners of twelve cotton mills. WOW! Not just my lucky day–my Guardian Angel. I am still so excited; I can hardly write this story. They were as fine a people as I have ever met. They told me to relax, be at ease, and we would all enjoy ourselves, the trip, and each other. That I would eat when they ate, and sleep when they slept. What do I do? Do I shout, sing, praise God, or pinch myself and wake up from this dream?

After a question and answer period about my life, my family, and my plans for my future, I was advised of their desires of my mission on the trip with them. I was to be a playmate for their son, and to keep him entertained. This turned out to be a real pleasure. He was quite a lad! Well-disciplined, respectful, and full of life with a wonderful personality. What a chore, ha! I don't know if I can stand it, this farm boy was about to go to town. I was treated like one of the family. They even had a thermos jug in the back of the car as well as goodies of all descriptions. I had never been in such luxury, and such ordinary people. An experience of my lifetime, of course, there were many. The Good Lord was really good to me, and had been for all of my life. And my Godly Mother had really been His helper.

We had pretty well gotten acquainted as we traveled down the road when he asked me how I learned to drive and if I had ever had an accident. Of course, I proudly related my experience. He was elated. So were his wife and son. They had never heard of such a fairy tale. In fact, he said, as he pulled over to the side of the road, "Please give us a demonstration," and he proceeded to get out of the car and insist that I drive for them. What a relief that would be. How proud could I be? Not only honored, but to feel that I could be of some help.

Well, I did most of the driving for the rest of the way. They were well pleased, and so was I. The Chrysler was appropriately named Airflow. It just literally flowed through the air, and to say the least, I was on cloud nine. I almost hoped I would never get to Phoenix. But we did—safe and sound!

We arrived at the motel and it was time to depart for me.

How do I say, "Thank you"? I am lost for words, believe it or not. The nice lady says she has the solution: "Let's not say good-bye. Meet us back here Saturday morning at 10 o'clock, and we will all go back home together." This sounded wonderful, and I still had all of my money.

So off I go from a favorable location on the highway where they drop me off. My luck remains good. I am gone almost before they get out of sight. But my expenses are all my own the rest of the way. My experiences are worth it all. I have never seen such sights or such displays. What an education. This farm boy is definitely in a dream world. I cannot conceive of all I see—much less be a part of it—but I never forgot Wofford or my education. It even became more important now than ever. I must become more than a country plowboy, and it is up to me and the Good Lord. He has blessed me so! Now, I have seen visions. I must not just dream dreams. My life must be more than following a mule behind a plow. If others can do it, so can I, and I'm on my way.

Needless to say, it didn't take long to determine that under my circumstances, money was flowing as though through the air. My mind was also flowing back to that Airflow Chrysler in Phoenix, Arizona, and a ride all the way back to Gastonia, North Carolina. I knew I had enough money to get me back to Phoenix, but did I have enough to get me back home to South Carolina? I checked my finances–my money–and it was already almost half gone. If I did not make it back to Phoenix in time to catch my friends, how would I ever make it back home to South Carolina? I called a family conference–I, Myself, and Me–and came to a quick opinion: If I had any common sense at all, I would exert all of my efforts to get back to Phoenix, hoping it was not already too late.

My luck hitch-hiking back was not nearly so good. It seemed as though I would never catch a ride. When I did, it was a short one. Time was fleeting. As I got closer, time got shorter. I wanted to catch a bus but one just would not pass. Just as I knew I was lost, along came a through ride. He just wouldn't drive fast enough. I finally told him my story, and he had a question for me, if he broke the speed limit and was caught, was I going to pay the fine? The time of departure was at hand and we were still trying to find the motel in Phoenix. When, alas! There it was! And there was the North Carolina Airflow Chrysler ready for take-off. They were glad to see me–excuse me–I was glad and thankful to see them. They loaded me up, and we took off for home. As expected, the trip home was wonderful. I drove most of the way. My friends dropped me off at my sister's place in Charlotte, North Carolina. I thanked them profusely and tried to tell them just how much they had meant to me. They seemed to understand and thanked me for my efforts, complimented me on my driving, but most of all told me what a good job my Mother had done with me. My mannerisms, my conduct, my entire personality were all so very commendable. They left telling me to contact them when I graduated. They surely could make a place for me.

From Charlotte, I returned to Spartanburg to reopen a business that I had started the summer between my sophomore and junior classes. As the results of my business contacts and ventures, I had learned that an ice cream factory had discontinued its operations of an ice cream parlor in the front part of its factory. I had met the owner several different times at different business meetings. He became very interested in me and my efforts to get an education and expressed to me his personal feelings and commended me very highly on my efforts and successes. I went to see him at his office and made him a proposition: I would help him advertise his business and increase his profits if he would lease me the front of his place at a price that I could afford. Thereupon, he volunteered to do better than that, he would give me the use of the space in the front of his factory, free. He would supply me with every flavor of ice cream he made–free–if I could prove to him that I was really what he thought I was, and that I would let NOTHING prevent my graduation from college. I graciously accepted his offer and his challenge.

Needless to say, he helped me every step of the way. He remodeled the place and made it into somewhat of a soda fountain, with ice cream, drinks, and all kinds of goodies. My specialty was the banana split. With free ice cream, nobody, not nobody, could match my three big dips of ice cream on my banana splits. I would also always push an extra little squirt of syrup in my cold drinks and fill the glasses with free ice.

What a deal! I was hardly opened before I could not handle my business. Word spread quickly of the quantity and quality of this new soda fountain in town. I had to hire new help, and business still grew. I had to hire more help– business overflowed me! I started curb service. Business boomed! I couldn't handle it anymore. I began to feel that I was losing money with the curb hop boys–collecting money and putting it in their pockets without checking back at the counter cash register. This I immediately put a stop to. When the curb boys came on duty, I gave them five dollars in change and required them to pay at the counter for what they served just like a customer would. They returned their five dollars at the close of the business day. This worked perfectly. Profits went up materially from a combination of business practices.

My incentive for the curb boys was free drinks, with order, for their girlfriend, and free ice cream for Mom and Dad. This became so popular and the word spread all over town and even more people came to support me and the business. They thought it was a nice gesture! I soon had to extend the courtesy to all of my helpers. Of course, the owner and his associates and special friends got royal treatment–anything and everything they wanted–anytime they wanted it. This was quite pleasing to the owner, and the exorbitant tips pleased the boys, and especially me. I never dreamed of such a business. The owner declared to me that it increased the volume of his business; thereby it also increased his profit. He was well-pleased.

On one occasion on a Sunday afternoon, we were really busy, and I was running out of Coca-Cola syrup with no way to replenish it, so I had to come up with some ingenious solution. I alone was to dispense the cokes. The plan was to use one-half of the amount of the Coca-Cola syrup and add a big shot of cherry syrup. This I personally tried and found quite tasty. I then tried it on the customers. What a response! I had more requests for refills than I had ever had. And the refills were the same price as the original drink. I give you my word–

it became one of the most, or *the* most, popular drink that I served. I told no one. But everyone noticed the difference. I told them it was just the Newton touch. It was so popular, that I eventually told them it was my Cherry Coke. And I served it until I closed. I truly believe that this was the very same Cherry Coke that the Coca-Cola Company sells today. It is still my favorite.

This business I ran two summers—the summer between my sophomore and junior years, and the summer between my junior and senior years (after I got back from R.O.T.C. camp and my "excursion" to California). The owner of the ice cream factory was so well pleased that he told me that he would gladly hire me to help him run his business when I graduated from college. However, he had nothing to offer to compare with what I was heading for. He thanked me for my help, enthusiasm, example and success. I, in turn, tried to explain to him just how much he had meant to me, and my appreciation. He seemed to understand.

PETER JACK NEWTON

CHAPTER 6

My senior year has arrived! I start early. I renew all of my business representations. My dry-cleaning jobs, my laundry jobs, my shoe repair job, my jewelry sales, and I continue my job in the dining hall waiting tables. I am now Mama Bear's Man. I usually serve almost all of the visiting ball players. I have become quite a professional. This pays for my room and board. I am also in advanced R.O.T.C. I am really quite a farm boy gone to town. I am really quite proud of myself.

I select my business associates for the above-mentioned jobs (keeping the best ones for myself) and sign up for my senior year quite in style. I pay off all of my college loans. I am debt free. This farm boy is now a free man. I have quite a bit more than $1.25 in my pocket, and much more than a pair of underwear, a pair of socks, and a pocket handkerchief in a brown bag.

Most of all, I am still Mama's Man. Next to that, I think I am the adopted son of the manager of S. H. Kress. They are treated better than a regular son, you know. I've got it made! In the manager's opinion, there is no other like me. He is my advisor, my counselor, and really quite my adopted Dad. Remember, I lost my daddy when I was four years old. There has never been another in my life quite like him. I am everything but full-time employed. I am his business partner. He takes me to all of the business meetings—says for training purposes. I get quite involved with the businessmen of the city. All of this is quite an education within itself for a farm plowboy. It is a totally new world. How wonderful it is to be here! No stopping me now! I'm grateful. I'm determined.

I sign up for a full course of subjects. This included calculus, a course in math that I had never known. This will give me a major in chemistry and a double minor in both math and foreign languages (French and Spanish). I had done well in all three subjects and also on my ministerial subjects. English, on the other hand, required too much time reading and reporting. I had to pay "brighter" students with more time to do my book reports, etc.

The Dean taught calculus. I had many personal sessions with him. He knew all about my efforts. He was definitely on my side. He thought that what I had done, and was doing, was quite exemplary and commendable! One day in calculus class, (which came right after dinner, and I had to finish serving tables, eating, and run to get to class on time), I was full from dinner, tired from work, and could not stay awake to save me. To shield my face and closed eyes from the Dean's view, I had put my feet up on the back of the seat in front of me. All of a sudden, I heard this gruff, stern voice call out, "Mr. Newton! Take your feet down so I can see your face!" This sudden command scared me half to death! Professors usually didn't bother. If you were not interested, they seemed to care less. You would just "bust the course". So, the Dean told me at the end of the class to remain a moment. I knew I was a "cooked goose"–probably expelled from class! The room emptied. I remained. The gruff, stern Dean became a wonderful man. He explained to me that he had admonished me because he had a special interest in me and wanted me to stay alert and pass his course. After a few moments of pleasant exchanges, he excused me.

One other special "confrontation" I had with the Dean was a bit more serious. I had requested permission to go to Charlotte on business. The request was denied. The "business" was to go to Guy Lombardo's dance to which a girlfriend had invited me at her expense! Well, again, all work and no play makes Jack a dull boy. I have a friend take me "clear out" (all the way) to the Charlotte side of town to hitch-hike to Charlotte. Once I got there, I had no problem. The "lady friend" had the automobile and the cash.

You will not believe this! I had hardly said thanks to "my friend"–she was not even out of sight when this nice car pulled up beside me. He asked no questions. He already knew! He didn't even ask where I was going. He already knew! He was the DEAN of Wofford College! He just said "Hop in." And we took off. Silence for quite a while, then general conversation. "How was I doing in school?" "Was I passing all of my classes?" "What was I going to do when I graduated?" "Did I have, or was I going to have, enough money to pay all of my expenses to graduate?" He was commendable of all of my efforts, and what an example he thought I was for any young man. And he explained what he had heard of my character and my personality. And then. . . "How was my social life?" At this point, I was ready to say, "Just let me out at the next stop sign, and I will be on my way home!" But before I came up with any answer, he continued that "He was quite fascinated" at all of my "business ventures", including my boldness, my techniques, my determination, and especially my successes. He understood that I was quite a professional waiter in the mess hall, a new prospect for S. H. Kress, a future Army officer, and had established quite a "lively" business at the ice cream soda fountain. He then informed me that he had visited them all and was really impressed! He was sure the dry-cleaning business, the laundry business, the shoe repair, and the jewelry business were all secondary. "By the way," he asked, "How many employees do you have?" "Are they all on commission?" "What percent do they get?" Finally, "Who is your banker?" he asked with a big chuckle. Somehow, he seemed to know the story of my life!

We are finally in Charlotte, North Carolina, at the Darling Shoppe, where my sister worked. As he pulled into a parking space, he had some final instructions for me. He proceeded to tell me that he is speaking at the Methodist Church Sunday morning at eleven o'clock and expects to see me in one of the first ten pews. After service, he would go to dinner with the church officials. He would then pick me up about two o'clock, and we would head back to Spartanburg. My only comment was, "Yes Sir, Dean. I'll be there!" And I was! You should have heard his sermon! I will say no more.

He was at my sister's at two o'clock sharp, and we were on our way. The conversation was normal, but slow. As he approached the very spot in Spartanburg where he picked me up, he commented, "This is where I found you; this is where I'm leaving you." And so, he did. Before he departed, he informed me that "This is where it started, and this is where it has ended—No in-between! Do you understand? And no here-after!" "Yes, Sir. I understand," I replied. There would be no punishment. The incident was never mentioned again.

No, I was not expelled. What a man!

This farm boy is now a dignified Senior in Wofford College! I am everything a college senior is supposed to be. I am confident. I have the greatest self-respect! I am respected. I attend business meetings, I attend church regularly, and for once in my life, I have some free time! I enjoy football, the Y.M.C.A. (Young Men's Christian Association), the college functions, and yes, now I am quite a social character! I am in "hog heaven". I can put into practice some of the lessons I learned from my older brother, Harvey, in my younger days. I not only learned them well, I remembered them well, and I performed them well! I was considered quite a lady's man for one year in my life. And I had free money to enjoy it.

I knew life had its problems, but I was not quite ready for the one I was about to face. It was time for mid-term exams, and all bills had to be paid before you could take your exams. I had collected all of my accounts, and so had all of my representatives. They had all paid their bills and collected their percentages. So off to bed I went the night before exams the next day.

I was up early the next morning. I had served tables and completed all of my chores. I was ready to clear with the treasurer. But, alas! My entire "stash" (cash) had been stolen during the night! This farm boy, this dignified Senior, this confident young businessman was totally lost and totally confused! It was impossible for me to come up with this kind of money. I rush to see the treasurer. I get all kinds of sympathy and agreement to assist with college expenses, but no way to become involved with personal or business expenses or finances. I made quick calls to the business establishments I represented. They admonished me and expressed great surprise–and surmised that they might have expected as much from a Senior. I was never so insulted, shocked, and deepdown hurt. But it seemed that some others, before me, had pulled somewhat similar stunts. Shall I tell it like it was? I was completely LOST!

I am back in my room in Carlisle Hall. It is time for exams to have started when the phone rang. It was for me. It was my "Girlfriend"–the girl I had called which had broke me up with my real Sweetheart. I had called her earlier when I found out my money had been stolen. She was inquiring as to my status and my plans. What was going to happen to "us"? My answer, to say the least, was not too encouraging. In fact, it was almost a sad good-bye. She said she would see me before I left for home.

It is some time later, and as I continue in my frustration, the phone rings again. It's for me again. This time it is the treasurer of the college telling me that all my bills had been paid, and that the Dean had arranged for my late entry into the first exam. The Good Samaritan was to remain anonymous. My mind went wild! Of course, I had my opinion! That kind of money was just not available during those depression days!

I went to my exam with much more on my mind than chemistry. It would have been more appropriate if it had been Bible IV. Oddly enough, the answers to the questions came rather easily. It was my favorite subject, if you remember.

Exams are over! I did really well! Semester break! I immediately went personally to see each of my business associates. I told them my story. They all seemed skeptical but apologized profusely for their distrust. Each denied being the anonymous donor, but almost all of them gave me a good bonus, complimented me on my business ethics, and asked me to please continue to represent them. This I gladly agreed to do!

It is now time for my girlfriend to fess up! This is her story: Her little 7-year-old brother had gotten really upset, had gone and gotten his piggy bank, brought it to her, emptied it out, told her to take it all and carry it to Peter Jack, and tell him "that will solve all his problems." I "can pay him back later".

This story she takes to her older brother and gets the same offer. This she adds to her stash and takes the total to her Mother with the story of the donation. She and her mother then go to Dad for his approval and the necessary balance. Then to the treasurer's office! And the subsequent phone call to me. Such action on such a scale completely floored me! It also humbled me beyond description. I had never felt so honored, so trusted.

I know that you know the rest of my senior year was quite an experience for this farm boy. He must now prove himself to be a "man" for sure! I was more dedicated and determined than ever to prove to my Godly Mother, my high school teachers, the gentleman who carried me to college, all of my business associates, Mama Bear, the Dean, my college professors, the manager of S. H. Kress especially, my high school sweetheart, and my special college sweetheart I had hurt so badly, and again especially my present entire benefactor family, that I was "everything" that they had helped me to be!

The final semester of my senior year passed so quickly that I could hardly believe it! We were preparing for graduation with all of its pomp and pageantry, all of its social life, and our future adventure out in the business world. First, I must clear up all of my business in my present world. We, my associates and I, started early and closed out all of our business ventures. We reaped a bountiful harvest! The day I graduated; I had paid everybody every dollar that I owed. And I had five hundred and twenty-five dollars still in my pocket. This included paying back my entire benefactor family. What a day! What a life! What a world! How the Good Lord had blessed this man! I shall forever continue to thank HIM! And to seek His guidance! One prayer answered was that my mother was able to attend my graduation. What a proud, thankful, day in my life. I was all of twenty years old!

Jack – Wofford College Senior

I went home with my Mother, as an honor to her, proudly displaying my college ring. Mother was proudly holding on to my college diploma. Going back home was to be quite an experience. Everything seemed to have changed. . .as it should have, I guess. After all, it had been four years since I left home. The farm life this country boy had left as so innocent was most assuredly extremely different from the life to which this educated city man had become accustomed. I found myself extremely proud of the farm boy I was, and even more proud of the educated man I had become. I was so thankful to Almighty God, my Mother, and all of my above benefactors and associates for this jointly produced product. In my mind and heart, I vowed to never let them down. I continued to ask God to be my helper. Until this day, at age eighty-nine, I must proclaim, "How God has blessed this man!"

CHAPTER 7

I must press on. A girlfriend I had met some time ago invited me to visit with her at Pawley's Island, South Carolina, as a part of my graduation celebration. She lived in Georgetown, South Carolina, about twenty miles away. Her family owned a hotel there, and it would cost us nothing for room and board. This was too good to pass up, so off to Georgetown I go—still hitch-hiking. This trip became a "big point" in my future life.

International Paper Co. had just constructed the biggest paper mill in the world there. The girlfriend read my mind and suggested that I go to the mill and get a job. Out to the mill I go. I determine that Mr. Harry Cotton is the Personnel Officer. I go in, address him, and introduce myself. The interview is underway. He seems quite impressed, well-pleased, and thinks Mr. Herb Martin, the Chief Chemist, will have just the place for me. He informs me that Mr. Martin is a Chemical Engineer graduate of The University of Miami. We need to send him a few introductory statistics. My full name, my address, my phone number, my age, the college I attended, and of course, the fact that I had a Chemical Engineering degree. "No, Sir! Just a B.S. degree in Chemistry," I corrected. "Whoa!" he exclaims, seemingly in great surprise. "Mr. Martin is presently hiring Chemical Engineers." He had assumed that I was aware of this fact. You've got that right—that was the sudden end of the interview. But it was not the end of my effort.

I left Mr. Cotton in his office. But instead of heading for home, I headed straight for Mr. Martin's office. Once inside that huge mill yard, I asked sufficient questions to find the Chemistry Department and the office of the Chief Chemist, Mr. Herb Martin. Yes, he was in. I introduced myself, and we got right down to business. He, of course, assumed that Mr. Cotton had sent me and got right down to the introductory statistics. When he came to the college attended, he spelled out W-O-F-F-O-R-D, and says, W-O-O-F-O-R-D. "Where the hell is Wooford?" to which I replied, "Where the hell is the University of Miami?" He giggled, thought that was quite smart, and stated that he "guessed that made us equally dumb!" We chatted right friendly for a short spell until he saw that I was not a Chemical Engineer. Things got completely quiet! He turned red in the face, looked me dead in my eyes, and asked, "Did Harry Cotton send you in here?" My answer of course was, "No, Sir!" "Then how in the hell did you get in here?" I began to tell him my story, and to my surprise, he listened intently. Then he asked me point blank, "What the hell made you think that I would hire you?" My answer was straight forward. "Sir, you are hiring other men on their degree. I am asking you to hire me on my ability. Hire me for thirty days, and if I don't produce as good as any man that you've got, then you don't owe me one penny." "Good!" he says, "I'll teach you a lesson. I'll work you for thirty days and save International Paper thirty days' pay!" He turned, picked up a rubber apron, and literally threw it at me, told me to put it on and report to the foreman on duty. He left me and went straight to the foreman for a lengthy chat; then called me over and introduced us and was on his way. All of a sudden, everything seemed really nice and business-like. I was assigned various duties and given every chance to make a mistake and hang myself. The Good Lord continued to bless me. The foreman was real special and was my friend, and helped me all the way.

At the end of two weeks, everyone was paid off except me. No comment! The next two weeks, I got along even better. I really thought I was as good as anybody. But, alas, payday again–thirty days–everybody was paid again, except me! Mr. Martin made sure he walked right by me, and into his office he went. But he did not go in alone. There were two of us! I went in right behind him. He turned and inquired as to what I wanted. I was never calmer, or more self-assured. I said to him, "Yes, Sir! I would like just a few minutes of your time." He says, "You've got it." I proceeded to thank him for the time he had permitted me to be employed by the biggest paper mill in the world. I now had experience that no one could ever take away from me. My future was now in my hands, and that I felt quite secure. He looked down on me with the kindest, approving, expression on his face, stuck out his hand, and said, "You have proven yourself beyond any doubt. You are MY man. Here is your pay for thirty days. Now get back to work."

Now for "the rest of the story": In six months, I was Foreman of a shift, and in eighteen months, I was Chief Analyst–second only to the boss himself, and his Assistant Chemist.

On shift work, you changed shifts every week: 7 a.m.-1 p.m.; 1 p.m.-7 p.m.; 7 p.m.-1 a.m.; 1 a.m.-7 a.m. If your relief on the next shift was sick, then instead of four, six-hour shifts, you worked three, eight-hour shifts–7 a.m.-3 p.m.; 3 p.m.-11 p.m.; 11 p.m.-7 a.m.; or pull a double shift of twelve hours. If you so desired, you could work an extra shift any time a worker was out. I worked double shifts (twelve hours per day) every time an extra shift was available. You remember, this was nothing new to me. And the extra time (overtime) pay was time and one-half. On holidays and breakdowns, the time was double time, with double pay. To me, that was a smart deal. You got twice the pay for doing the same job. As Chief

Analyst, not only was the pay better, I was on straight time 8 a.m. until 5 p.m. with Sunday off–all day-time work, except on shut down or break-down. I was "on call" then, twenty-four hours per day.

Yes, I had found my home! Four years in college, and eighteen months with the mill, this country boy had moved up the ladder from plowing a mule fourteen hours a day in the hot, dusty, sun for thirty-five cents per day, to the position of Chief Analyst in the biggest paper mill in the world, in a salaried position, in an air-conditioned, and steam-heated Chemistry department. Was I in hog heaven, or should I pinch myself and wake up from a Cinderella dream? "No!" I keep telling myself, "This is real!"

As you might expect, the lifestyle in this small town trying to survive The Great Depression is now unreal. There are literally hundreds of people swarming all over the town seeking food and lodging, and the other necessary essentials of life–almost like overnight. The big blessing was almost a big disaster.

My new home was with a lady and her son, Honker, and other roomers. We slept three in a bed. Honker and the other roomers also worked at the mill. We ate at a private home, turned into a boarding house. You had to pay today for your meals tomorrow, so the lady would have enough money to buy the food for you to eat. The arrangement was good. The boarding house was just across the street from where I was working. The next real blessing was that Honker had a car! He was a top-notch electrician. He was also on 8 'til 5 and on call at the mill. How lucky could I get? He became my closest associate–my best friend. What was his and his Mama's, was mine–including the use of the car–a new Plymouth. About two weeks after I was hired by International Paper Co. for good, I received a notice from Dupont to report for an interview, and employment if all went well. I have failed to mention that I had applied for a job with Dupont as my first choice just before I graduated from college. I thought they were tops!

Can you imagine my dilemma? By now, I think I am well-established with International Paper Co. At least, I feel that I am. I have an offer to report to Dupont; and I most of all want to be a Doctor, a surgeon in fact. My initial plans were to work two years and save all of my money and return to Medical School. Before I graduated, I had contacted several medical schools, and I had been offered a scholarship at Vanderbilt, at Emory, and at Duke. But, alas! All of my time would be taken in class and in lab. I would have no time to work, and I surely didn't have the money to pay my way! If I went, I wanted to be among the best. After all, being a doctor could mean the difference between life and death!

It's time for another family conference–I, Myself, and Me! I decide that I am already established at International Paper, and I had better not press my luck. After all, I was going to return to medical school after two years. Anyway, by now I am already involved with another venture. There was no agency for the *The Charlotte Observer* newspaper in Georgetown. But there is now! My agreement with the agent for the Georgetown area was for him to determine the number of papers he would send, and that I would sell all that I could for a commission, but I would owe nothing for the ones I did not sell if he sent too many. No problem! There were two papers available already: *The State* from Columbia, South Carolina, and *The News & Courier* from Charleston, South Carolina, but nothing like *The Charlotte Observer*! Again, I say, there was no problem.

I sold all the papers he sent. He sent more. I sold them all! He sent more, and I sold them, too. But there was a limit. It was unbelievable! It was time to hire an assistant. I then hired a route boy; then another; then another! All was going well—and continued to go well. My assistant was also my businessman. He kept books and did the collecting; but I continued to be the paymaster and banker.

I had started selling "Mason" shoes and boots in college. The money and business were so good that I continued at the mill. The boots were as good as, or better, than the money. I wore them all the time. "Sell ten pair—get a pair free", plus the commission. Then sell the FREE pair. It didn't really make any difference where the money came from, as long as it was honest. Anyway, I was a walking advertisement. Everybody liked them. (I'll still get you a pair today if you want one real bad.) I still have two pair in my closet—a black pair and a tan pair, and I'm eighty-nine years old! Ha! They are my favorite; and they are so-o comfortable.

All of this time, I never ceased going to church, if and when my work permitted. Neither did I ever cease going home to check on my mother, usually about once a month. It was also my policy to pay all of my bills on time. I never used credit. I learned early on; it can ruin you. I had one bad problem—I found it very difficult to refuse a fellow worker a short-term "disaster" loan. They lived from paycheck to paycheck. The men would hock their shotguns, etc. The wives would hock their sewing machines. Can't you just imagine me taking their sewing machines?

I have passed right by one of the deals of my life. I had to have a car. Beginning with my very first paycheck, I saved every dollar I could. I checked the price of a '38 Chevrolet Deluxe—cash on the spot—in Georgetown. Then I called the dealer in Columbia for the same deal. I was quoted $60 cheaper. The deal was on! I hitch-hiked to Columbia to save enough to buy gas to get us (my new Chevy and me) back to Georgetown. Everything went as planned, except better. When I paid the dealer in cash, he had the car filled with gas for me— FREE! This permitted me to strut around town for a spell when I got back.

PETER JACK NEWTON

CHAPTER 8

All was really going well for this now educated farm boy. But I have completely neglected to keep you up to date on my social life. When I left college, I was totally beholden to my girlfriend and her entire family. After all, they were responsible for me being able to stay in college and graduate on time. I could NEVER forget that. She was still my "Special"! New location brought new friends, however—male and female. One of my male friends had a very special girlfriend that worked in the 5 & 10 cent store, and he insisted that I just had to meet her. So, I did. She was a beautiful creature! She lived at Pawley's Island and depended on her daddy to get her to and from work. Many times, he was late picking her up to take her home. Her boyfriend would sit with her or she would stay at a girlfriend's house until her daddy came for her. Things were about to change.

Her boyfriend, and my male friend (same guy), asked me to please take her home when Daddy couldn't make it, or was really late. He would pay me. After all, I had a brand-new car, and working 8 'til 5. I was always available. When I was late, she would walk a couple of blocks to my landlady's house and sit on the front porch with her until I came. Alas! Disaster!

My "Special" was going to Winthrop College at this time and was rooming with the daughter of the lady who ran the boarding house just across the street. Now, don't jump the gun! Just stay on board! The daughter came home one weekend and observed the activity described above. She could not wait to get back to Winthrop! When she did, she told everything "in her own words". You would never guess what happened the next weekend. My "Special" came walking up to my front door about four o'clock on Saturday evening. She had come down on the bus. She had already stopped by the 5 & 10 cent store. She had already made up her mind! I was completely lost. She was heart-broken. She cooked my goose–overtime! This irked me to say the least.

To make things worse, if that was possible, I was to take the girl from the dime store home at six o'clock. My "Special" knew me to be "too much of a gentleman" to leave the lady on the street when I told her I would take her home. So, when I asked her if she would like to go with us or stay with my "house mom", she firmly told me, "Neither!" She came on the bus and would be leaving the same way! So, I did my best to accommodate her desires. We took off to the bus station but found nothing going her way until the next day. But a bus was leaving from Sumter about 100 miles away at eleven o'clock. I offered her a choice: I would either take her to the hotel, or to Sumter to catch the bus since she said that was the way that she "would be leaving"! Her answer was so sudden that it shocked me. "Take me to Sumter," she shouted! I kept both of my promises. I carried the girl home from work, and my "Special" stayed with my house mom. Then I carried my "Not-so-Special" anymore to Sumter. When we parted, we stayed parted. There was no reprieve.

I told my 5 & 10 cent store girl what had happened. She lovingly placed her arms around my neck, placed a kiss on my cheek, and assured me that she would NOT be a replace-ment. She would be even better than anything I had ever had before! That was quite a promise. But she lived up to her promise, and then some. We went everywhere together. We did everything together. We grew closer and closer. I was quite at home with my 5 & 10 cent store Sweetheart. She was just as sweet as she could be and had an hour-glass figure. She was indeed a "Pretty Lady". She keeps telling me about this special girlfriend that she has. She's closer than a regular sister—more like a twin! They grew up together, went to school together, played basketball together, and had even worked in the dime store together. Her special friend's Uncle and Aunt ran a restaurant out of town. Their main helper had gotten sick, and they needed help really bad and quick. This special friend, sweet little Ethell, tells her boss. He understands and tells her to go with his blessings—but to hurry back. Well, guess what? Ethell is coming home for the weekend. What a special event!

Speaking of special events, Guy Lombardo and his Royal Canadians are coming to Charleston for the big Azalea Festival Celebration Dance. Well, my Sweetheart knows we are going—she and I and my new car. We've just got to get Ethell a date and take her with us. So, I get a nice young man from the mill for her date. And to the Guy Lombardo Azalea Festival in Charleston we go! By now, you must know that Guy Lombardo was my all-time favorite band. If I had any jitter-bug, or shag or devilish dance in me, he would bring it out. My Sweetheart and Ethell did their part to bring it out as much as the band did. Sad to say, but Ethell's date from the West was no match for these southern jitter-bugs. So, I had two of the prettiest, loveliest, dancing-est ladies that I have ever met to keep entertained.

Being The Gentleman that I was, that Mama had taught me to be, and that I thought my Sweetheart would have me be, was about to get me into trouble! I admit that I probably paid Ethell more attention than I should have. I made sure, however, that I danced the last number—"The Waltz You Saved

For Me"–with my Sweetheart. That was my custom. But my Sweetheart just did not seem the same. This attitude rode with us all the way back home. Ethell was in the back seat having a ball. At times, I found myself wishing I was in the back seat with her!

I found out later that the reason Ethell was home was that her folks had closed the restaurant. She went back to work at the dime store the following Monday. I had double trouble! When I went in the store to flirt with my Sweetheart, Ethell would flirt with me. Another problem–Big problem! Ethell lived in Andrews, South Carolina, eighteen miles away. My Sweetheart lived on Pawley's Island, twenty miles away in the opposite direction. Please come to my rescue. Since they worked together, how could I not take Ethell home, too? After all, I had a new car. One of the few in Georgetown. And I was on all day work–8 'til 5–at the time. The dime store did not close until 6 p.m. and after all, she was my Sweetheart's lifetime best friend.

I will save you all of the ensuing gruesome details. My Sweetheart got jealous. I could never figure why. She had conflicting plans one Sunday night, so I ride over to Andrews late that Sunday afternoon (just out riding, of course) and stop by just to say hello to Ethell. She is not at home; in fact, no one is at home! I stop by a girlfriend's house, and she tells me Ethell has gone to a huge tent revival out in West Andrews. Whoa! By the way, Ethell is engaged to Buddy from Hemingway, and Sunday night is his night–so is Wednesday and Friday. So what? I'm engaged to my Sweetheart, and any night is my night, (except, of course, tonight). Well, I ride out to the tent meeting. What a massive crowd! I had never seen the like. It looked as if every single seat was filled, and people were all on the outside. I cannot explain to you why, but I get out of my car and start walking around the back of the tent, from aisle to aisle, looking down the aisle toward the pulpit when, bless my soul, I spot Ethell!

What is more–there is a vacant seat right beside her. But there is a young man sitting on the other side of her. Even though I figured she was with him, for some unknown reason, it did not deter me one bit. Down the aisle I go, wiggling my way down the bench behind her. When I get to her, I lean over and whisper, "Am I intruding?" She looked over her shoulder with her big brown eyes and devastating smile, inches closer to the gentleman beside her, and beckons me to come sit beside her. Do you believe I did just that! All through the service, I sat by her side knowing that the man on the other side was not Buddy, but not knowing if he was her date.

At the close of the sermon (what a dynamic sermon), there was an altar call. Ethell immediately sprang to her feet and took off to the altar. During the singing and the praying, I could see Ethell just weeping and wiping her eyes and her nose with her little bare hands. Just as if I had been ordered to go, up I went and knelt down beside her and slipped her a clean pocket handkerchief (remember, I always had one). As she took it from me, she pressed my hand tightly, dried her eyes, and attempted to give it back to me. Instead of taking the handkerchief back, I took her hand in mine, and we prayed together. The preacher kept coming by telling her everything was alright now–until I informed him that he had done his part; the rest was up to her and The Lord. He agreed and departed. When Ethell was ready, we went back to our seats. This is when I was introduced to her brother and his wife. He was the man seated beside her!

When the service was over, she introduced me to her mother and father, and inferred that I would be taking her home. Her mother seemed well-pleased, and we followed her parents home. I parked in the little driveway, close up beside her house, right outside the bedroom window. I'm sure Mama kept close watch on her child. We didn't mind!

We talked together until two a.m.! It was alright with Mama—she thought I was one of the preachers. We told each other our life's story. You know mine. Her's was quite fascinating. She was one of eight children—six girls and two boys. She was number five—after brother Alton (her Special). Brother Duke was my Special. More about them later.

Their family home for both Mama and Papa, was in Mullins, South Carolina, about fifty miles north of Georgetown. They had moved to Andrews (also about fifty miles from Mullins), where they owned and operated a sawmill. Both Mama's and Papa's families were farmers. Their main crop was tobacco. Buddy was also from a farm family from Mullins. They were all country neighbors. As children, they worked together, played together, went to church and school together, and quite often ate together. They all helped each other—even in the tobacco fields and at the tobacco barn, especially on "puttin' in" days. That's when you would crop the tobacco leaves, string them on sticks, and hang them in the tobacco barn to "cure". You would then remove the cured leaves from the wooden sticks, "grade" them, tie them into bundles, and take them to the tobacco markets, where they would be sold at the big tobacco auctions. Her dad had traded his part of the family farm to his brothers and had bought and operated the sawmill. He moved his family to Andrews because of the huge timber lands. They cut the huge pine trees by hand, "snaked" them to the sawmill with mules, and cut them into lumber for sale. Now you can get the connection. Buddy had continued his relations with Ethell quite seriously. He was in Andrews about three nights a week.

There was one trouble with the courtship with Buddy. He was definitely no drunk, but he would drink now and then. This Ethell could not tolerate, especially for a husband, nor for a father for her future children. Now you can get the connection here—Buddy, the tent meeting (revival), Ethell, and Me. Ethell had begged Buddy to go to the revival with her that Sunday night when I dropped over to see her. He would not agree to go with her, so she gave him a choice: "Go with her to the revival or go home." He rudely chose the latter. He went home. And she went to the revival with her mom and dad. I found her at the revival.

We told each other literally ALL (everything about ourselves, family, etc.) that night! Let's figure this all out: My Sweetheart, to whom I was engaged (by understanding—not by pledge yet), had set me free. Ethell's sweetheart, to whom she was engaged (also by understanding and not by pledge yet), had set her free. Now, here were "we"! This could get serious. I knew Sunday, Wednesday, and Friday nights supposed belonged to Buddy. I was not quite so committed verbally. I propose a date for Friday night, quite boldly. She responded, Wednesday night. I jokingly give her a choice—"Friday night or Sunday night." She responds, "Friday night." She shocks my boots off. Then she sends me home.

We are both quite troubled to say the least; but life goes on. Our two counterparts had made the first bad moves. They had opened the door. Now a "bad storm" was about to "blow the house down". When Buddy came Sunday before revival, he was drinking. That was not good. He lost his temper. That was worse. Ethell knew that I did not smoke nor drink. (She tells me later that she began to make comparisons.) Buddy would not take her to church; I followed her to the altar. Buddy drank and cursed when he got mad; I never drank, and she had never heard me curse or be anything but a gentleman. She said that she believed she really felt the very depth of my soul!

Things rocked and rolled on for a while. My Sweetheart confided to me that she could never be to me what Ethell could be. We (Ethell and I) had so much in common, even the same farm background, but that she loved me more than any man she had ever met.

"Lightning strikes!" One Sunday morning when I was down on the street with the paper boys, this car passes me going North with my past Sweetheart (Ethell's best friend) in it with another man. It was her old sweetheart. They were on their way to get married! You will have to write the next paragraph.

I had started a new venture. I was selling apples by the truck load–bushel by bushel. My brother was bringing them straight from the mountains by the truckload, and I was selling them by the bushel at the mill. They were beautiful and delicious! A thought hit my mind: As I was filling the bushel baskets, I would pick out, apple by apple, the prettiest bushel from the whole truck load and carry them to Ethell. This I did. They were indescribable. But I carried a "special proposition" with them when I carried them to her. If she would be my date Sunday night, call me, and tell me to "Come get the old basket– she was ready for a new one. The old basket was empty and could be considered discarded!" But, if she was not to be my date Sunday night and EVERY night from now on, "Just forget the basket, the apples, and ME." I would trouble her no more.

She tells me later that she had prayed and asked The Lord if Buddy was not the right one, to please make her know it in no uncertain way! She said that all the answer she got was

"I've shown him to you!" She said that over and over again she prayed, and over and over again she got the same answer, "I've shown him to you!" So, she had gotten out of bed and gone to her Mother and told her about her prayer, and her answer, and asked her what she thought about it? She said her mother's immediate answer was, "I believe if I were you, I would call that young man and tell him to come and get his 'old' basket; that you had 'discarded' it, and that you were ready for a 'new' one!" And that they had laughed and cried together. *What do you think of her prayer? What do you think of her answer? What do you think of her mother's answer? What would you have done if you had been in her shoes? What do you think of me? (Please don't answer that last question so anyone can hear you!)*

What a wonderful, and I think, "God-sent" answer came over my phone: "You may come Sunday night and any night that you would like to come. Apples or no apples! The basket is empty! Every night from now on is your night–our night, if you so desire. It would make me really happy." It was Ethell's voice on the other end.

What an exciting moment in my lifetime! I can't express it here. You will just have to imagine it for yourself. What a proposal! What an acceptance! The old was gone–discarded. We were ready for a new life together. And so, it was from that moment on until February 20, 1996, when the Good Lord called her home. We had literally lived for each other–together for over fifty-six years. I don't believe any two people were ever happier, more dedicated, more devoted, or more contented.

Ethell – about 19 years old

CHAPTER 9

Well, things began to happen so fast, I don't know if I can record them. My mind was NEVER so much at ease. I NEVER felt so sure. I NEVER felt so confident. We felt like the Good Lord had saved us for each other! We seemed to understand each other's every thought and move. There NEVER developed any doubt! Not for fifty-six years!

Ethell gives her five-and-dime boss notice of her engagement and termination. I give her my college ring for an engagement ring. This I had never done before. We began to look everywhere, all of the time, for our new home. We shopped for apartment furniture one piece at a time. We got our bedroom suite from my sister Ada. It was beautiful! A bed, a vanity, and a chest of drawers. I still use it today. It's been sixty-six years. I had given Ethell's family a refrigerator from Sears Roebuck right after the revival. Mother Rogers was determined we must have it. So, we took it for ours, and gave her a new one (Granny wasn't too dumb either). We bought a four-eyed "Prosperity" gas cook stove and a table and chairs from Sears to complete the actual needs. An apartment, a bed, a cook stove, a refrigerator, and a table and chairs.

Yes, by this time, we had found an apartment. We already had it furnished and we were ready to move in. It was real nice and cute. Upstairs—one bedroom, one kitchen/dinette, one living room/den, and a bathroom. To this we added a real nice "Warm Morning" pot-bellied heater. A fenced-in back yard was made available to us. We used it for our chicken yard.

In the meantime, we visited a real good friend—a member of the South Carolina House of Representatives (politics) that owned and operated a General Merchandise Store in Andrews, South Carolina, (Ethell's hometown). He also represented a jewelry firm in Columbia, South Carolina. Our purpose there was to buy Ethell a diamond engagement ring. He said they sold the best in large or small carat. He said he would get us one at cost for our wedding present. So, the deal was on!

By this time, we had set the wedding date: November 29, 1939—Thanksgiving Eve—at the Methodist Church in Andrews. However, that was not to be Our Wedding Day. Franklin D. Roosevelt, the President of the United States, had moved Thanksgiving up a week to November 22. He said, "for economical reasons." But the real reason was he knew I couldn't wait! (Ha!) So, we moved the wedding up to match—if the diamond ring would come in on time!

During this time, we had also completed another urgent preparation. We had gone to Charleston, South Carolina, and bought Ethell's wedding outfit. She found what she said was the perfect outfit—but a-b-s-o-l-u-t-el-y unaffordable. So, I assured her that if the politician could give her the diamond at cost, I could certainly give her the wedding outfit as a wedding present. So, the deal was on!

One other problem—My dad was dead—I wanted my brother Duke to be my Best Man. Well, guess what? He was getting married that same night—"secretly". And couldn't accommodate me. He said, "turnabout is fair play." He wanted me to be his Best Man, also! Well, we both got married the same day, the same hour, 120 miles apart. He confided to me that he had also sent President Roosevelt a directive to move the holiday up! I can't truly say that our reason for moving the weddings up was for economic purposes.

Oh, I forgot to tell you the diamond came in! It was truly BEAUTIFUL. It sparkled like a full carat on display. It was on display alright. On My Darling's finger. It was hers! And she was mine (to be).

The wedding was on. Trinity Methodist Church in Andrews, South Carolina, November 22, 1939, at 8:00 o'clock in the evening. Everybody came. But Duke and Lib! It was everything you could want it to be for a Country Boy and a Million Dollar Baby from the 5 & 10 cent store. A couple of little incidences did occur, however. The preacher stumbled as he came down front and almost fell. And we left the keys in the car while we went in the church to get married. What a mistake! When we came out, of course, there were no keys in the car! Peter Jack surely was not that dumb. The caring, concerned pastor came to question what the trouble was. At this time, he needed to be concerned about my soul. The Good Lord, however, had sent him with a very appropriate question. "Don't you have a spare key?" he asked. Of course, I did! It was almost a new car. So, to the reception we went. What a wonderful occasion! Until it was over, and we started to leave for our Honeymoon. Our special friends had an unheard-of surprise for us. When we got in the car, cranked it, and put it in gear, it did not move. No matter what I did, it did NOT move. Our special friends had jacked it up, put a board right beside and behind the rear tire, and let the jack back down "almost" to the ground! You could not tell that it was even jacked up! But all it did when you put it in gear was spin the tire. I never felt so stupid. My friends finally jacked it up, removed the board, and let me down. And off on our honeymoon we started, or so they thought, with a convoy (motorcade) behind us!

We went through town, around town, around and around trying to shake them. Little did they know that we planned to spend our honeymoon night in our own little apartment. All of a sudden, we found ourselves all alone. To our apartment we went. Here we found the surprise of all surprises. As we opened the door, and I picked my beautiful bride up in my arms to carry her across the threshold—I dropped her! Literally! A BLAST of intense heat overwhelmed us. I yelled at her for the first time, "Stay here!" And up the stairs I went, through almost blistering heat, threw open the doors and windows, and slammed the vent shut on a RED HOT, big bellied, Warm Morning heater. And back down the stairs I went—feeling totally blistered—and slammed the front door shut to prevent a draft. Praying and waiting. And watching for a blaze—which thankfully NEVER came.

Shutting off the vent stifled the burning coal, and the cold Thanksgiving night air eventually cooled the big stove and the entire house. Needless to say, we have spent the rest of our lives giving thanks to Almighty God for His blessings.

When we eventually got upstairs to stay, one of the things we had to see was where the intense heat had drawn the tar out of the pine mantle, and it had dripped just past the red hot stove pipe. If one drop had hit the hot pipe, the house would have been gone. One thing is for sure—We had a "RED HOT" honeymoon and a time of giving thanks.

The reason for the near disaster was caring, helping friends. One friend had started the fire. He had it going. Then he filled the big heater with coal and closed off the vent, so it wouldn't burn too fast, or get too hot. Then another friend came by to check to be sure it would be cozy warm when we got home and thought it was smothered—so he opened the vent to get the fire going, thinking we would be home any minute (real soon). The hot coal flared from the new draft, and we did not come home in time to cut the vent back, and it took off full blast. Thus, the situation when we arrived.

Off we go into the wild blue yonder the next day—heading to Asheville, North Carolina, to the Battery Park Hotel, The Biltmore Estate, and a tour of the mountains. Ethell had never been to the mountains, and it was going to be my pleasure to give her the tour.

We were cruising along full of love and emotion, about twenty-five miles up the road, when *BANG* went an explosion. I almost wrecked the car trying to hold it steady, thinking I had a blow-out from a tire. I got the car off the side of the road to put on the spare tire. What? There was no flat tire. I checked the motor. I cranked it up. I shut it off. I cranked it up again. I shut it off again. Everything was normal. What do I do now? Do I dare drive it on further from home? Do I try to get it to the closest shop? What do I do with my precious bride? We decided to drive it on. It ran perfect. We decided it was some prankster trick! After driving about twenty-five miles per hour for about twenty-five miles, we tried it back at normal. Everything continued well. There was never any trouble!

About six months later while sitting at the dinner table at Ethell's home one Sunday, her favorite brother, Alton, questioned about a "sudden explosion" at any time during our honeymoon trip? I sneakingly acted surprised, and told him, "Every time I kissed your sister!" He proceeded to tell me that he had thrown a spark plug torpedo (a type of fireworks) up the tail pipe, and wondered if it had ever exploded? Ethell and I both "exploded" all over him! That was his answer. Now we knew the answer to our mystery. When the tail pipe got hot enough, it exploded the torpedo. No damage—except to Alton!

Well, on to Asheville, and the Battery Park Hotel. When we ventured out the next morning, everything was wild. In the lobby. In the street. On the roof. There had been a murder in the hotel some time after midnight! We were temporarily detained, then permitted to go. What a honeymoon! Ethell said she expected excitement, but not that much, and not that kind! The rest of the honeymoon was terrific. I finally became The Main Attraction, The Man of the Hour! It was up to me to match the competition. I never was satisfied to play "2nd fiddle".

Finally, we are back at home in our own little apartment. There is no doubt–I am Man of the House now. Ethell is The Queen. And what a Queen she is. She is my Beauty Queen, Miss Personality, Miss Congeniality–Mrs. Peter Jack Newton! And THAT she was for fifty-six years.

Pawley's Island was immediately added to our *Charlotte Observer* paper territory, and I gave it to Ethell, along with a paper boy. She was superb! She really enjoyed her competition with the *The State* paper from Columbia, South Carolina. She just about put their paper boy out of business. Until my venture, there had been no *Charlotte Observer* in Georgetown nor Pawley's Island. So many of the people that came to the beach and that had come to the Paper Mill in Georgetown were from all over the country. The little business had become quite lucrative! She sold her papers at the beach by the paper.

Life is wonderful. My position at the mill is a dream come true. Since I can't seem to become a doctor as I had hoped, having Ethell as my mate for life is better than having a doctor's degree. She also seems to be almost in heaven on earth.

Our lives settle down and become quite routine. We are only eighteen miles from her mother and dad, and 120 miles from my mother, so we keep check on them on a regular basis.

I truly believe my Mama loves her as much as any child she has and Ethell just helps her ENJOY her life in her own style at her own pace. She doesn't try to baby her, to be a nurse maid, to boss her, or tell her what to do, nor where and how to do it! She loves her so much. She just tries to help her be herself. And Mama loves it to death.

Ethell & Jack -1940

PETER JACK NEWTON

CHAPTER 10

E thell and I are so HAPPY, so devoted, so much in love!
It seems too good to be true! And so, it is!

The mailman brings me a "Call to Active Duty" in the U. S. Army. To report for duty February 26, 1941. I was to report for my physical at Fort Moultrie, South Carolina, and then to proceed to Camp Claiborne, Louisiana, to join the 367th Infantry Division.

These Orders were from the War Department. Of course, I followed, leaving my precious wife behind and alone–almost. She was pregnant! How tough can it get? At least The Lord had helped us to provide an established home in Georgetown for her and the baby. I was so thankful for that!

I reported as directed to Fort Moultrie for the physical, passed it with no limitations, and preceded to Camp Claiborne, reporting to the C.O. (Commanding Officer), ready for duty. I had gotten my uniform and necessary supplies from the post clothing store. (Officers have to buy their own clothing and supplies. The government supplies all the needs of enlisted personnel.)

What a SURPRISE I got. Camp Claiborne was a Tent city. On top of a red clay hill, which meant it was full of red clay mud when it rained. I was assigned as S-2 (intelligence officer) on the Regimental Staff. All of our officers were white. All of our troops were to be black. They had not yet arrived.

I understand that the officers were from the South. The enlisted men were from the North. I also understand that this is to be an Experimental project. We officers were told that we were to handle the troops with white kid gloves. There would be no distinction at any time at any place. Eat together, sleep together, bathe together, fight together, die together!

Captain White, the Regimental S-3 (Plans and Training Officer), and I (the S-2) were assigned Temporary Limited Duty (TLD) to Fort Benning, Georgia, to attend a six-weeks' Officer refresher course. We would leave for Fort Benning just as the troops were arriving.

The school was a life-time experience all by itself. It taught you how to live instead of die, if possible; how to defend and how to attack; how to become an expert in the use of your weapons; how to gather and use intelligence; map reading and supply; marksmanship and first aid; discipline and leadership—and so much more. You literally had West Point in six weeks.

Now comes the break of my life. At the end of the course, instead of returning me to Camp Claiborne, General Omar N. Bradley, the Commanding Officer of The Infantry School (and later General Eisenhower's right-hand man in World War II), kept me at Fort Benning to help start The Officer's Candidate School (OCS). Also kept were Captain Frederick, Captain Pickens, and three West Pointers—Lt. Col. Coursey, Maj. King, and Maj. Todd. (Again, this is not for record. If there were others, at my age, and mental status, I don't rightfully remember.) Maj. Todd was my C.O. I believe Maj. King had three officers under him. Col. Coursey was the head man. We were all under Gen. Bradley.

I started with Officer Candidate Class #1 in early 1941 and stayed with the school until I believe it was early 1944. The graduates were commissioned 2nd Lieutenants and called 90-Day Wonders.

Application requirements for the OCS were Leadership Qualities. The finest men in their unit were to be chosen. They were sent to Fort Benning OCS for the most rigorous, most intensive, most demanding, most condensed training feasibly possible. Again, four years of West Point in ninety days! Only the best were to be chosen. I (each officer) had fifty candidates under my command. My decision, at the end of ninety days, determined whether they were commissioned or failed the course and returned to their home station. I literally lived with them. I was at their disposal for guidance, counseling, and advice. Twenty-four/seven. Their future was in my hands! It was truly the greatest responsibility placed on my shoulders that you can imagine. Each soldier that I commissioned then became the Commanding Officer of the enlisted men in the U. S. Army in the future. How many times over would my decision, my efficiency, my judgment be multiplied? I had fifty! That fifty would have fifty more. Immediately that would be 2500. And no way of knowing how many in their future, as they advanced in ranks. I literally gave 100% of myself and any more that I could muster! There was no limit to my sincerity.

These candidates were the country's BEST! And they proved it on the battlefields. I was so honored, so proud, to be a part of their lives. Without a doubt, they brought out the best in me.

Class after class they came. They were commissioned 2nd Lt.'s and sent straight to the battlefront. I was promoted to 1st Lt. and then to Captain. Now I am Company Commander and have 150 candidates. Responsibility increases and so, does my family.

Jack "Climbing Ladder of Success" upon promotion to Captain
Photo provided by 161st Signal Photographic Company

One of the GREATEST events of my life occurred July 15, 1941. My precious, beautiful wife gave birth to our first child—a beautiful reproduction—a 7 lb., 9 oz. baby daughter. She was born at the Fort hospital, and we named her Alice Jacquelin. Ethell came up with the name. War seemed imminent, and there just might not be any more, so—Alice came from Alice Ethell (her Mother) and Alice Cleveland (her Grandmother), and Jacquelin came from Peter Jack (her Daddy) "A.J.N.". Everything went well. Mother and daughter were in the hospital nine days. When we started to check them out, we got quite a shock. Our bill was $9.25. How could we afford it?

The Good Lord had blessed us again and again. After my assignment to the OCS at Fort Benning, I had rented a house in Columbus, Georgia, nine miles from the Post, and brought my wife to me shortly after I was assigned to stay with the OCS. So, we had a home to bring our baby to!

Jack in Columbus, GA

What a blessing we did not really know until we met, and became a part of, our neighbors—Hugo and Ess Brandt. They had three small children. Frances was the oldest, then Punt (Eleanor), then Judy. They were life-long residents. No finer people have I ever met. They took Ethell and baby Lynn into their lives as though they were their own. But as stated above, my life was almost totally consumed with my officer candidates. Training all day and guidance and counseling at night.

Life rushes on! January 4, 1943, brings another GREAT event into my life. My precious, beautiful wife brings another precious, beautiful daughter into our family, again at the base hospital in Fort Benning—8 lbs., 2 oz.—eighteen months after the first. Ethell had read this beautiful Bible story in which Ronna Claire was the main character. Thus, the name of our new baby daughter! Everything went well. Nine days later, on schedule, we checked out of the hospital. We got another shock. This bill was $9.50. Ronna had cost us twenty-five cents more than Lynn!

Was she really worth it? Ha!

Then the Real Shock! I received Orders to Report for Duty with the 78th Division at Camp Butner, North Carolina (near Durham) about the first of 1944. This I did, leaving the dearest things in the whole wide world to me at Fort Benning—my wife and babies, and my mother in Newtonville, South Carolina (near Bennettsville) at the Old Home Place. Ethell was pregnant again with our third child. What a dilemma. My entire life was changed. That was for sure. I did not have a home for my wife and babies, and I was sure I was headed overseas in combat with a unit in which I did not know a single soul. Can you imagine the turmoil in my very soul. If you can't, I can't describe it.

The 78th Division was called the Lightning Division and was commanded by Major General Parker. When I reported for duty, I was assigned to the 311th Infantry Regiment, commanded by Col. Olmstead. He in turn assigned me to the Third Battalion of his Regiment as Battalion Executive Officer (2nd in command).

My position is now Battalion Executive Officer of the Third Battalion of the 311th Infantry Regiment of the 78th Infantry Division. But only for a short while. My Battalion Commander is assigned special duty, and I become Battalion Commander. There are three Battalions in a Regiment. This places me second only to the Regimental Commander and his Executive Officer, alongside of the other two Battalion Commanders, who were Lt. Col.'s. (Lieutenant Colonels)—Professional Officers, U. S. Army—I would say at least fifty years old or older.

WOE is me! Here I am twenty-seven years old and a Reserve Officer and almost equal in rank (holding equal position). Double Jeopardy! I am also a trained graduate of the most modern, professional infantry school in the United States. Trained in the most modern combat tactics straight from the battlefield. I should be a MOST DESIRED addition and a GREAT ASSET to any outfit. This I was to Col. Olmstead, the Reg. C.O.–BUT, instead, I was considered a THREAT to the old professionals. I was immediately ostracized, with no cooperation or mutual assistance. Col. Olmstead recognized this, and the reasons why, and told them that we should all benefit from my expertise and modern training. This seemed to make it worse. Even the Col. was showing favoritism.

And so, he did. He made me his Reg. Exec. Officer, which put my position over all of them–second only to him. They out ranked me, but my position placed them Subject to My Orders. This position I retained while I attempted to the best of my ability to bring all of the officers and staff up to date on modern warfare tactics as taught at T.I.S. (The Infantry School–Fort Benning, Georgia).

This was the best thing that could have happened to me, for me. The Colonel explained to them that the better we were trained in the most modern tactics, the more lives would be saved in combat, and the more successful we would be. Then I became Rudolph, the Red-nosed Reindeer. I gave them my best. They responded well. The Colonel then reverted me back to my position as Bn. C.O. (Battalion Commanding Officer). I was still just a Major with the same assignment as two old Lt. Col.'s. This still left some friction, but not nearly as much.

I had hardly arrived with my new outfit with my new assignment with my own Battalion, when off we go to Camp Pickett, Virginia, and Tennessee Maneuvers, preparatory for overseas deployment and combat in the ETO (Eastern Theatre of Operations) in France, Belgium, Holland, and Germany. Things were happening so fast, and there was such a change in my assigned duties for combat instead of training, that I could hardly keep my mental balance. My family, my future, the welfare of my troops. My pregnant wife, and two baby daughters, my aging mother. But I NEVER doubted my leadership. My training had been superb! Gen. Bradley was my idol. My training under him and my contacts with him were overwhelming and the challenge of my life. His confidence in me, followed by my experiences with Col. Olmstead, played a key role in my future life!

Lt. Col. Lipscomb, a West Pointer, is assigned to our Regiment and is assigned to command the 3rd Bn., which is my outfit. We now have a Lt. Col. commanding all three Battalions. This reverts me, a Major, to Bn. Exec. We finish maneuvers and go into combat with this staff.

Combat overseas was now definitely in my future. Contact with my family surely is over, or so you would think. But it wasn't. My precious wife insisted on coming to me. So, I secured a small, dilapidated farmhouse in the vicinity of Camp Pickett, and "HERE she comes," a very much pregnant wife and two baby girls–to be alone. Except occasionally. To be with her man EVERY POSSIBLE fleeting moment before he left for overseas–and life or death in combat.

What an experience was to follow. Baby Ronna fell off the bed one morning and lost her breath. Ethell frantically tried everything she knew, but to no avail. She finally threw her on the bed and literally jumped straddle of the child and started jumping up and down on the bed shouting and praying for the Good Lord to save her child, and He did. Ronna went from rigid to limp. Ethell thought she was dead.

Then she began to breathe!

It wasn't too long after this that Ethell had another call. This time, it was her new baby knocking (kicking) at the door.

Literally saying, "I'm coming out—ready or not!" This was no hide & seek! This was for real! So, to Richmond, Virginia, to the Medical College of Virginia she goes on the third day of July 1944, to a Dr. Hudnell Ware late in the evening (leaving the girls with a babysitter she had secured).

Well, Dr. Ware informs Ethell that he doesn't work on the 4th of July for anyone. So, they deliver the fine, healthy, pretty, baby BOY (8 lbs., 8-1/4 oz.) before midnight on July 3, 1944. We are in the Staging Area preparing for overseas deployment at this time, so there is no Leave of Absence permitted; but I DO get to see my (our) boy before I ship out to New York and on to England on the plush ship Acquatania. My brother Roy comes to Virginia to get Ethell and the kids and carries them home.

There was never any doubt about the baby's name if it was a boy. It was to be Peter Jack Newton, Jr. (another "P.J.N."), if I did, or didn't make it back home. Ethell made sure of that. She would still have a Peter Jack with her for the rest of her life. And if I did come back, she would have two! MERCY! How would she EVER handle that? But I did come back! And she handled it well. (Until Libby married one of them and took him off her hands) Libby says, "They are just alike, but I (she) got the best one!"

CHAPTER 11

Overseas we go! Shortly after we leave New York Harbor, Pier 86 (I believe), we pick up a German submarine, or it picks us up; but with greater speed and maneuverability, we eventually lose it! On to England, and to LeHavre, France, where we landed at Cherbourg, on Omaha Beach at Normandy.

The Allied Forces were clearing the hedge rows, and securing the landing, and making the March on Paris, France, when we joined the combat forces. What an experience passing through Paris! We established our first combat in Aachen, Germany. The Hertgen Forest was where I received my first wound—shrapnel on the left knee. But it drew no blood, so I weathered the wound, mostly in my Jeep. I remember it well! It made me so mad; I personally wanted to kill the whole German Army. I was quickly advised, however, by an old Sergeant, to settle down before I got myself killed. He informs me that there are enough Germans out there for us to kill 100,000, and still have plenty left. So, we started on that mission. Not in order, but I remember especially Düsseldorf, Cologne, The Swammanual Dams, The Majinot Line, The Roer River, Simerath, Kesternich, The Rhine River, Remagen Bridge, and Huppenbroich, to name a few!

I shall not attempt to record here the action or battles of our outfit. History has them recorded many times in many places. But I will attempt to give you a brief synopsis of my final days in combat. The Good Lord had blessed me well.

One of the experiences of my lifetime was during a snow-storm. My Jeep driver and I were checking the troops when *CRACK* came the sound of a rifle–we thought. We later found out it was two rifles that had been fired simultaneously from snow-camouflaged positions. One bullet came through the windshield directly in front of me–I felt my body jerk! The driver's body literally rose from his seat, taking his foot off the gas pedal. I instantly slammed my left foot down on the gas pedal while he held the steering wheel until we were out of danger. We then stopped the Jeep to see how bad I was hurt. I could feel the blood running down my chest. I opened my coat–No blood! I opened my shirt–No blood! I checked my wool undershirt–No blood! My entire body was clear of any wound or blood. What had hit me–and where–to jerk my whole body? The bullet had actually gone between my left arm and my chest and hit the metal plate in the middle of my pistol butt, denting the metal and busting both sides of the handle! My pistol was hooked onto my web belt which was strapped around my waist and my shoulders. This accounted for the terrific jerk on my body! No! My body was not touched by the bullet. There was no blood. Just vivid imagination.

Now for my driver. What caused his sudden reactions? Here's his story: "Now, Major, that you see you're not hit"–and he starts pulling down his britches–"how about seeing how bad my 'a . .' (butt) is busted!" The bullet from the second gun had gone through his rear-view mirror and traveled between "his seat and his meat," literally branding the back side of both cheeks! But–No Blood! I sent a combat patrol back to take care of the snipers!

One other incident probably never reported. My outfit was dispatched up the Rhine River to secure the Remagen Bridge (which had been captured intact) and to clear the opposite side of the river to assist the main crossing of the Allied Forces. I understand that this bridge was the only bridge on the Rhine not blown up. It was left as a morale factor for the last Germans who were defending the Rhine River to cross when they retreated.

Our troops were loaded on trucks and proceeding to the Remagen Bridge with the flaps down. We went through town with the stop lights still working. As we were traveling through some woods, we began receiving machine gun fire straight into the truck convoy just above the heads of the troops. When we captured the two guns, they were manned by Belgium gunners strapped to their guns and guarded by a German SS Trooper. The reason we were not slaughtered. The Belgium gunners had purposely, and unbeknownst to their captors, beat on the backs of the guns with the base of their hands, and any means possible, just enough to elevate the barrels to fire the bullets just above the heads of our troops in the trucks. When we captured the SS Trooper, we asked why he had surrendered. His answer was, "I have served my Fuehrer well in combat, and I will continue serving him in your Prisons of War camp!" For some reason, I understand, he never enjoyed that privilege.

On to the Remagen Bridge we went, across it, securing it, and proceeding down the other side to complete our mission.

We were on our way to Berlin. It had to be just a matter of time. We were all beginning to sense the taste of victory. How long could it be? Then the final answer came!

I was wounded the last time on the thirteenth of March 1945, in Rheinbreitbach, Germany, on the Elbe River, just short of Berlin! I found out later that we should have already been in Berlin, but it had been decided by the High Command that the Russians should have the privilege of going down the streets of Berlin first. I was hit in the back of my right hand, almost severing the entire hand. The hand was severed between the knuckles and the wrist all the way over from the little finger to the last blood vessel coming down from between the index and long finger, and the thumb and wrist joint. It was severed right up to, and against, the last blood vessel! If it had gotten that last blood vessel, there would have been no possibility of saving the entire hand. As it was, most of the right half of the hand was missing. The tendons of both the little finger, and ring finger were severed. Blood was gushing everywhere. The Good Lord's guidance and His God-given instinct saved my life. I tried to cover the hole in my right hand with my left hand, but the hole was too big! I first tried with my fingers of my left hand closed, and the blood flowed from each side of my hand. I then spread my fingers, and the blood flowed from between each finger. While attempting to adjust the finger spread to permit the least amount of blood flow, I passed out from the loss of so much blood and fell to the ground. The Good Lord directed my fall and positioned my body flat on top of my two hands clasped together. This applied pressure on the mostly closed wound, and the seeping blood clotted between my fingers and the sides of my hand. This stopped the loss of any further blood!

When they found me there was no more bleeding! So, they took me as I was to the Battalion Aid station. They listened to my story in disbelief but agreed that I should go to the General Hospital in LeMons, France, as I was. But before they shipped me off, they gave me a blood transfusion and a shot of Penicillin (a brand-new drug to keep down infection). Penicillin had just arrived in the Aid station for the first time that very day. How the Good Lord did bless this man! When I arrived in LeMons, France, at the General Hospital, they could not believe what they saw. There was no infection! Not even any redness about the wound. So, another shot of Penicillin and another blood transfusion!

Then the conference of three Doctors—whether to take the hand off at the wrist or at the elbow. The consideration of possible blood poison and the length of time since the wound had also been discussed. At this time another doctor steps in the picture and asked, "What have you got here?" The reply, "An amputation." Question: "What's the problem?" Answer: "Whether to take the hand off at the wrist or the elbow." Question: "The Colonel has made many decisions affecting other men's lives. Why don't you let him make this one concerning his own?" Just about this time, I am being given a shot of Sodium Pentothal and told to start at 100 and count backward. (I should have gotten to about ninety before I passed out.) But, instead of counting, I said, "For God's sake, Doc—Leave it on!" And I was gone.

When I awoke, my hand was still on. It was bent almost 90 degrees to the right! The stitches could not draw the upper and lower skin together. The wound was too wide. My hand was placed in a tray-like device. It was also placed in a whirlpool of melted paraffin many times a day to help the skin to stretch until the stitches could draw the skin together for permanent closure. Once this was accomplished, the next procedure followed. Still using the hot melted paraffin whirlpool, they would periodically (several times an hour), almost microscopically straighten the hand bit by bit. It took quite a spell, but the hand, wrist, and arm were eventually all straight in line.

Now for the cut ligaments of the little finger and the ring finger—they were attached to the ligaments of the long finger, so that when one finger was opened and closed the whole hand opened and closed together. What a deal! Miraculous! (Note here that I am handwriting this story of my life at the age of eighty-nine years with this miraculously saved right hand.)

My recommendation for promotion to Lieutenant Colonel was granted while I was recuperating from the wound to my hand. However, this wound automatically took me out of combat. I could not defend myself with the weapon with which I was armed–the 45-caliber pistol. I was headed Home!

Peter Jack Newton, U. S. Army

Because I was a walking wounded and could pretty well take care of my own personal needs, with my arm in a sling, I was scheduled to make the trip back home on a hospital ship, probably within thirty days. So, my barracks was my home for a while–or so you think. The airport was right beside the barracks. I could see the planes take off loaded with badly wounded litter patients headed to the States. Sometimes there would be one less crewman on the flight than others. This causes me to wonder about that empty seat. Why couldn't I fill it? In my spare time, I walk around to the Sergeant's desk, get acquainted, and pop the question, "Why couldn't I fill one of these spare seats one day?" To which he answered, "Be my guest!" If I could be ready at a moment's notice and catch the plane before it took off! The deal was made.

I wasted no time in getting ready and waiting for the call. I packed my bag–souvenirs and all–and waited for the count down. It was not long in coming. While lying on my bunk, I heard this call, "Col. Newton, Col. Newton, report to my desk!" I sprang to my feet, and out the door I went. As I rounded the corner toward the Sgt.'s desk, there he was waving me on to the waiting plane readying for take-off. Straight to the plane I went and got there just as they were about to take up the steps. The Sgt. had cleared my pass for the flight home. Off we go into the wild blue yonder headed for home. Whoa! I forgot my bag! Souvenirs and all. Too bad! They will ship it home to me–sometime! Well, they did. . .sometime later. But no souvenirs. The rear area Cowboys had helped themselves to them.

As we arrived over New York, President Franklin Delano Roosevelt's funeral procession was proceeding down the street below us. The Pilot tilted the plane to one side, then to the other, so that the litter patients could get a view of this passing history. When the plane had landed and the patients were unloaded and taken into the hospital, I was left in the hall on a stretcher. I was later loaded on a plane and sent to Finney General Hospital at Thomasville, Georgia, with only the Pilot and Co-Pilot.

This flight turned out to be quite unique and historical. As we flew over Richmond, Virginia, I pointed out the hospital where my son Peter Jack, Jr. ("Pete") was born, just shortly before my outfit was shipped overseas from New York. Then, as we proceeded south, kind of down Highway #1, I began to feel quite at home! My Uncle Melvin Newton had constructed a filling station at the intersection of Hwy. #1 to Rockingham, North Carolina, and the road to Hamlet, North Carolina, going south, and called it Newton's Point. Well, would you believe, I spotted it, and pointed it out to the Pilot and Co-Pilot, and assured them that I knew where I was. If they continued on course, we were going to fly right across my housetop. I began to beg for a parachute. I would jump in the field beside my home, and they could go to Myrtle Beach. The Pilot told the Co-Pilot to give me his chute and let me jump. "After all, my service for my country was over, and if that was what I wanted, so be it." The Co-Pilot thought for just a moment, and then tells me, "Col., I love you man, but you ain't getting my chute! Just as sure as I give you my chute, this plane will go down, and you'll be home playing with your wife, and my a... (butt) will be mud." By this time, we were about to fly over the housetop. Almost. . .but not quite. So, the Pilot gets on the radio to Maxton Air Force Base near Laurinburg, North Carolina, (about 17 miles from home), explains the situation, and asks what craft, if any, is in the air. His response was, "One plane." Pilot: "Get him down. I'm coming through." Operations Sgt.: "Yes, Sir! He is coming down. I'm all for it."

Surprise! The Operations Sgt. calls back to the plane on the radio and asks, "Sir, does the Colonel have a telephone in his home?" By this time, I have the earphone on my ears, and I give the Sgt. this reply, "Yes, Sgt., I do. Sen. Strom Thurmond had it installed for me before we went overseas." Sgt.: "Good.

Let's try something and see if we can make it work. What's your telephone number?" I tell him, and he explains his plan. He's to get my wife on the phone in our home on one end, and me on the radio in the plane on the other end. I talk to her over the radio—my voice will come out in his office—loud and clear—he puts the telephone receiver by the radio speaker. My voice goes over the phone to my wife at home. She, in turn, speaks to him by phone, and he relates the message to me by radio. Sounds simple enough! From plane to Operations Sgt. to wife at home by radio through plane; from wife at home through phone to Operations Sgt.; from Sgt. to husband on plane by radio. "Good! Let's try it!" I shout.

The procedure starts. The phone at home rings and rings and rings. No answer. Sgt.: "Sir, there is no one at home." My response: "Sgt., There has to be! My mother does not live alone. My wife is there with her and three babies." At this time, we are flying directly across the top of the house. The Sgt. replies, "Yes, Sir, we'll try again." And he did. My wife answered the phone, and the Sgt. explained the plan. My wife exclaims that she understands (and I'm sure she did! Ha!) Of course, I am hearing the Sgt.'s half of the conversation. My voice will go straight from me in the plane to her in the house. Her voice would go to him by phone and then on to me by radio. Now comes the Sgt.'s voice to me: "O.K. Col. Ready—Go!" When I say, "Hello, Darling", but all I hear is the Sgt. trying to answer my very excited wife that I can't hear, "Follow the plan!" All settles down. Do you believe that? Well, somewhat. I explain to her that I have just flown over the housetop, headed for the hospital; that I love her so-o much; tell the three kids and Mama that I love them; and hope to see you all soon! What a thrill! What excitement! By now, I am well on my way south to Georgia to the hospital. I am so excited talking to my precious wife that I can hardly stay in my britches.

I found out later why there was no answer to the phone at first. Mama was in her room rearranging furniture and had the bed against the door and couldn't get out! She was calling to Ethell to answer the phone. Ethell couldn't hear her or the phone. She was in the outhouse (the outside toilet) watching the plane go overhead. I told her I knew where she was. She had left the door open and I could see her! Whereupon she immediately covered herself with a covering gesture of her hands and proclaimed, "You didn't do it!"

Before I go further, I must tell you of the nation's reaction on Armed Forces Day soon thereafter. There was this story of a wounded officer flying home from combat and flying right over the housetop of his wife, mother, and children. And talking with them from the plane over the radio and through the phone to them in their home!

Seemingly, it was the first time this had ever been done. We got phone calls from everywhere!

I arrive at the hospital, Finney General in Thomasville, Georgia, and continue the intensive therapy on my hand. I am also started on treatment for my badly ulcerated stomach, and therapy for Anxiety Reaction for my brain (emotional) and nervous system, and a diet to try to put some weight on my skinny body. By now, I can write quite legibly with my left hand.

The doctors say that I am progressing, but slowly, especially with my ulcerated stomach and my anxiety reaction problem. My flash backs have gotten worse and are causing great concern. I holler in bed and spring to the floor seeking cover and become quite emotional when help arrives. Past memories, in dreams, are not too desirable. I am prone to cry at any time. This, to say the least, is not too manly, but I am so thankful to Almighty God that my condition is no worse that I literally refuse to let it get me down. It is somewhat embarrassing, however, to both me and my fellow man. Everyone is so responsive and so sympathetic. But they just don't understand. And the problem is, "There is no way to explain it to them!" And I do not try. Again, I say, I am just so thankful to Almighty God that it is no worse. Again, I say though, that it is bad when you can't pray, praise, speak of peace, or joy, relate stories, or listen to stories, without crying—in public, or when you are alone.

CHAPTER 12

Finally, at last, I am permitted to go home. I catch the train to Hamlet, North Carolina, the closest stop to home. Ethell meets me there with Lynn and Ronna. Pete stays home with Granny Newton. When I get to the car, Lynn is quite receptive, but Little Miss Ronna is backed up in the seat corner as far as she can squeeze. But with Mama's assurance, she finally comes out with a big, sweet greeting. My crying does not help any, of course. Needless to say, there is quite a scene on the street. Then home we go. The same thing at home. Granny has Pete in her arms to present to me, and there I am—in my Mama's arms. What an experience in one's life. Mama, of course, trying to take care of her baby's hand.

Then the rest of the family, church, and community. How much better can Heaven be? I was always proud, but I don't think I was ever so proud. How could anyone ever be worthy of all they were making over me? This Country Boy–Lt. Col. Peter Jack Newton was HOME. How could he be a Colonel and only thirty years old? My Daddy would surely have been proud of me, too. In fact, to tell the truth, I was indeed proud to be a NEWTON. And at this time, I was proud to be PETER JACK NEWTON, LT. COL., U. S. ARMY, from Newtonville, South Carolina.

All was well, until Ethell went out to feed the chickens, feed the hogs, and milk the cow. This was a "No! No!" for Peter Jack. For his lovely, beautiful, sweet wife to have to milk the cow, switching her long tail full of cockle burrs in Ethell's beautiful face, was just not to be. I don't know who I thought had been doing the milking all the while, but at least I was not going to just stand there, looking on, while she did the milking. So, Lt. Col. Newton orders his Lady up from there, to yield the bucket and the stool. Gee! I hope this cow has respect for my rank and my uniform. Also, I had not considered milking all four teats, about two gallons of milk, with just my left hand. I started proud and doing just fine with my left hand, but not being used to it, it didn't last long. I just plain gave out. But admit it? NEVER! I decided to try to strip the milk from the teat with my thumb and forefinger of my right hand. At least I could stall while my left hand rested. I could just feel Ethell looking at me and laughing, "Goody, goody, you aren't the man you thought you were, are you?" But when I looked up at Ethell, tears were just flowing down those pretty cheeks from those beautiful brown eyes. This did me in. Forget the milk; forget the cows; let the calf have the rest of the milk. But Miss Ethell smiles through her tears, encourages me, and suggests that we need about a quart more, and then let the calf have the rest. This last quart I would have milked if it had taken me all night. Ethell knew this well. She just didn't want to see me whipped and give up. She knew this would literally kill me. We had enough milk anyway. But you've got that right–again. Too bad for the calf. Between milking and stripping, I milked the cow dry. Then I got my pay. "I knew you could do it! I knew that you would do it," Ethell says as she hugs my neck and cries.

Milking the cow

Well, I had three weeks of sick leave, and I don't have to tell you, I milked the cow every day of it. At first my hand got real sore, but then it got some better. It still really hurt, but, oh, it got stronger and stronger. My therapy at home was to almost constantly squeeze a tennis ball that they had given me to keep in my pocket. This I had done almost religiously.

Three weeks sick leave was gone almost like a day. Back to the hospital I went. The first morning back in therapy, I got more attention than I expected. Everybody was excited. No one could believe the condition of my hand. What had I been doing to it? Whatever it was, I couldn't stop now. I informed them that they had one of two choices—bring a milk cow to the hospital or send me back home to my wife and our milk cow. The decision was immediate. Back home I must go. And I did. For six weeks' sick leave and milking therapy. Then again. And again. My recovery was almost miraculous—in so far as it was possible. But there was no feeling—the nerves were dead from my long finger to the right side of my hand. I would drop things from the right side of my hand and not even realize it. But I was so thankful to Almighty God that I still had my hand. By now, I could do a pretty good job of eating with it. I could also spank my wife with loving love pats. That is, when she wanted me to.

Ethell was not only my adorable, precious wife; she was my God-given Angel. She encouraged me to do everything, and anything, I could do to improve the use of my right hand and give me confidence. And then rewarded me with a special love that was worth all the effort.

As for the ulcerated stomach, she became my special, personal dietician. And her efforts to keep me calm and secure were indescribable. There is just not an institution, nor a special attendant, nurse, nor doctor, that could do for me, and mean to me, what she did. Her love, and tender loving care, was worth more to me for my anxiety reaction and personal needs than the institution, medicine, doctors or nurses at that time. I have always thought that my nerves, and anxiety, and uncontrollable reflexes had more to do with my ulcerated stomach than diet. So be it! I could, and will, continue to praise her until I die. Then there was my precious, Godly Mother, and our three children, playing their role in my new life on the old family farm! How much better could Heaven be for this country boy? I could go on forever. My wife, my children, and my mother were my life.

I must admit that at the age of eighty-nine years, six months, I have great difficulty in recalling events, places, and names in chronological order. I spend much time trying to bring things back to memory in proper sequence at the proper time. I do not apologize for this. Instead, I thank God for blessing me by helping me forget so much of the undesirable. He has helped me completely wipe them out of my mind. Especially the actual combat. Much I will not attempt to recall or dare to record. These comments here are not intended for recorded history, but for recorded events to the best of my memory.

Speaking of forgotten events—my commitment to, and time spent at, Halloran General Hospital at Staten Island, New York, is like a blur on my memory. I think what helped to get me there was my automatic, instantaneous reaction when an airplane would break the sound barrier and make an exploding noise, or a firecracker would explode very close to me. I would fall to the ground like I had been shot, by natural instinct. This to me was like an artillery shell, or mortar shell, or bomb from a plane. And my best protection was to be the smallest target possible. As soon as possible. It was like real, live combat, and life or death was at stake. I did not understand all of the experiments or special protective treatment that I received at Halloran, but I am sure it was all for my benefit. I tried to the very best of my ability to cooperate with the entire program. My stomach was still a major problem. But so was my anxiety reaction. I was still in therapy for my hand, but its condition was almost miraculous, although it was dead—no feeling in it on the wounded side.

I believe I left Halloran General worse than I was when I went there. All of the protective measures they took in my behalf really increased my anxiety. In my cell, there was no seat on the toilet. They were afraid I would purposely break it and hurt myself. When I bathed, an attendant would hold one end of the towel while I dried my body. This was to prevent me from hanging myself, or choking myself, or whatever. And so on.

Then a private interview—just the Psychiatrist, me, and a guard for safety purposes. I never expected what was to come. But all was for my benefit, I am sure.

A short time later, I received orders for six months T.L.D. (Temporary Limited Duty) at Fort Benning. Would you believe? I'm back Home again! This limited duty is to give my body—my brain, my stomach, and my hand—time (and time was badly needed) to heal, and to readjust, if possible, to my present-day life.

I was assigned to The Tactical Section of T.I.S. (The Infantry School). I was to share my experiences on the battlefield with the instructors and be of whatever assistance I could be to them. This was one of the best assignments I ever had. Everybody did everything, in every way they could, to help me to adjust to become a real man—a real Soldier—again.

One of the greatest experiences of my entire life overwhelmed me. My precious wife and three babies joined me in Columbus, Georgia, for my Tour of Duty at Fort Benning. We were able to rent a house right beside one of our very best friends from our previous Tour of Duty at Fort Benning with the OCS (Officers Candidate School). The Brandts were our neighbors. They became more than that. They were like our parents, and our kids' grandparents. They practically adopted Lynn and Ronna. Hugo was the outside grill cook and the grounds keeper, as well as the Chief Baby Charmer and caretaker. Ess was the inside hostess. Ethell was her Little Princess. I don't think they could have loved each other anymore. Frances was the Nurse, Babysitter, Little Mama. Punt and Judy were the little playmates. We practically lived together. Everybody loved little Pete. They all made a fuss over him all the time. I guess Ess had first claim on him!

This Country Boy was now truly in hog heaven. I don't know how anyone could have asked for more or better. But I did. And, Oh, What a wonderful little package SHE was! I should have known better than to go back to Fort Benning. Here is where my first two were born. They were both girls. Lynn and Ronna. It was about nine o'clock in the morning. I was already on duty at the Fort when I get this phone call from Ethell in Columbus—about nine miles from the Post—calling for transportation to the Post hospital. Now! The baby was on its way. At that time, you didn't know if it was boy or girl until it was born. I rushed to my C.O. (Commanding Officer) Col. Passileague and requested permission to go to my wife. She was having a baby. I give you here the answer that I got: "Sir, I know that it is necessary for the daddy to be there at the 'lay of the keel', but he ain't worth a damn at 'the anchoring'!" Then after a chuckle, he tells me to be on my way, and to stay until my wife wants to "get rid of me–which should have been nine months ago."

Mother did well. And daughter, Patricia June Newton (yet another "P.J.N.") was born without any difficulty, weighing in at 8 lbs., 2 oz. A pretty, sweet, smiling (and quite a little pistol) Baby Doll. And she has been that way ever since. They were in the hospital nine days, which was the usual stay if all went well. Home to Columbus we went, to join the crew with our addition. The hospital bill at the Military Post Hospital was $9.75! Lynn had only cost me $9.25 (7/15/41), Ronna $9.50 (1/4/43), and now "Tricia" $9.75 (3/13/46). Mercy me. I can't afford to have any more children. It's getting too expensive. I think I will return Mr. Pete. He cost me $350.00. He was born at the University of Virginia Hospital at Richmond, Virginia, just as I was leaving for New York and overseas. Of course, he was born July 3, 1944, just before July 4th. I guess that cost us extra, too.

Fort Benning was truly my first choice of any of the Service installations. However, I must say, and I do proudly say, that the U. S. military, its officers, and enlisted personnel, its institutions–hospitals and recreational–and all of its service personnel were all extremely nice to me. I was extremely proud to be one of them. The discipline did not even bother me. My mother might well have been one of their training staff. Just do your best. That is what was expected of you.

This situation could not go on forever. The war was over. There must be some disposition of me. I thought there still might be some place for me. I applied for a Regular Army Commission. At present, I was only a member of the R.O.T.C. I was ordered to appear before a Regular Army Retirement Board. They knew all about me! They had all of my records, both Civilian and Army, and proceeded to literally display my Service

Record in front of me. They were extremely lavish with their praise and complimented me on my entire service life and what they knew of my civilian life. They all said they would be glad to have me join their Rank. They expressed their feelings that at my age, and my Rank, Lt. Col. at age thirty, and only a reserve officer–not even a West Pointer, I surely should have a bright future in the military–especially in the Army.

BUT, my physical condition. . .And they proceeded to evaluate that condition.

My ulcerated stomach–which did not seem to want to be healed.

My anxiety reaction–records and evaluation were not in my favor.

My wounded right hand–which would not permit me to defend myself with the weapon with which I was armed (the 45-caliber pistol).

These were three reasons that would not permit them to accept my application for a Regular Army Commission. But that any one of the three was sufficient to send me into retirement for physical disability. Therefore, I was to be Retired on three counts for: No. 1–Ulcerated Stomach, No. 2–Anxiety Reaction, No. 3–Wounded Right Hand. They then preceded to each one shakes my hand, thank me for my exemplary service, my shed blood, my dedication, and my offer to continue to serve. They expressed their congratulations for my Rank of Lt. Col. at the tender age of thirty and wished me well for the rest of my life.

I was ordered to Pratt General Hospital in Coral Gables, Florida, to continue my therapy and recuperation. What an assignment. What luxury for a Country Boy! How good can it get? Such I have never experienced before. From here I will be retired. Why must I leave? Just send my wife and four babies to me here. Since that can't be arranged, I'll just have to go. I sincerely hope with all my being that nothing, not nothing, will ever separate us again.

Special Orders were eventually presented to me: "That I was hereby relieved from active military duty this twenty-ninth day of June 1947, for physical disability for wounds received in action." That I should "proceed without delay" to my home in McColl, South Carolina, etc.

These Orders put into action previous arrangements for my precious wife to come to beautiful Coral Gables, Florida, for a "Thank you, God" celebration for my safe return home and reunion with my most precious wife and babies, and my mother—and everybody else!

I reserve the next paragraph to myself. Use your own imagination. It will work.

PETER JACK NEWTON

B ack to the farm—the place of my birth—to my most precious wife, our four babies, and my wonderful mother. The place where I started, BUT now quite a different man. From a healthy Country Plow Boy to a wounded—not so healthy—Lt. Col., U. S. Army. My stomach will forever hurt. My mind is quite troubled. I live in constant fear that I might have a violent reaction and hurt someone, or even myself. I hated firecrackers, or any sudden change of noise or action. I especially feared even the thought of a blow out of a tire on the car I was driving, or passing, or following. I feared my reaction to the sudden explosion might endanger someone. Your life or death depended to a great extent on the way you reacted, and the speed with which you reacted in combat. The mental anxiety and constant fear are certainly not desirable. Neither is it quite describable.

Then add to the above a wounded right hand that is greatly reduced in use, and numb to a great extent, and so dependent upon to even eat, or write, or work, and you might see a little reason for some anxiety.

But let it be known to my precious wife, caring mother, my young innocent children, or to my friends and neighbors—NEVER was I too proud, too thankful. My great desire was to be a real man. Definitely NOT a weakling. I would even catch myself looking in the mirror to see if my pain or anxiety showed. I would literally almost burst trying not to cry in the presence of anyone. This turned out to be impossible. And it still is today. My cup just literally runs over. I cannot talk, listen, or tell stories without being sentimental. But I am worst of all when I am alone–with my thoughts and memories and thanking Almighty God that it is no worse. I thank Him. I thank Him. I thank Him. For the blessings that He has bestowed on this man and his family. I shall NEVER cease to give Him PRAISE. Still now at eighty-nine years old, I don't believe you will ever hear me complain. I will discuss the situation and give you my opinion, pro or con, but I don't believe you will hear me complain. If the situation gets too bad, I have the answer to that: "To Hell with it! It ain't worth it!" If I can handle what I've been through, I can surely handle that. I will respect your opinion, and then proceed to ignore it for my own benefit. I try real hard not to get too upset. It would really not be too good for any of us.

I start my NEW life DETERMINED, and trying my best to be a good man, a good husband, a good dad, a good son, a good neighbor, and a good friend. And thanks to Almighty God, I'm still on that same course today–fifty-nine years later and eighty-nine years old. God being my helper, I NEVER plan to change. I am happy. I am satisfied. I am contented. And I am ready when God calls.

As I have said before, my precious wife left this almost Heaven on Earth at Fort Benning, and Columbus, Georgia, to come home to my mother on the farm to be her personal companion and caretaker and share her personal concern for their man. No electricity, no lights, no running water, no inside toilet, no electric heat, and no air conditioning. No electric stove, no electric refrigerator, no electric blanket, no TV, no electric washer, dryer, iron, or any other modern convenience. All of which she had at Fort Benning.

But she surely had a wonderful Mother-in-Law's LOVE, respect, and admiration for the rest of her life.

All of this is so-o-o nice. But I must get back to work. I could have returned to my position with International Pulp and Paper Co. in Georgetown under normal conditions. But I am not normal. I am told that because of the condition of my right hand—partially severed, and partially numb—I would be a danger to my fellow man handling the dangerous caustic and acid chemicals necessary for my profession. Therefore, I could not be re-employed. What a deadly blow!

My hopes, or any plans I ever had of being a doctor, went down the drain when I was called into Active Duty with the Army. My ambition to make a career with the military was blown with my wounded status and physical disability. Now, my civilian career with such a bright future is shot. And now, too, I have a wife and four babies, and an aging mother, and questionable health. What next?

I had asked The Good Lord to be my guide. I could not distrust Him now. I had passed my twenty-first birthday. The farm was still intact and had to be divided. Five of the older children had already received their share of the estate when the part of the farm in Laurel Hill, North Carolina, was divided. That left the South Carolina portion to be divided between the four younger children and Mama. My sister Vida sold her share to brother Duke who had become married and established in Columbia. My brother Roy bought my sister Lucille's share. She was married and established in Pensacola, Florida. I had bought brother Duke's interest—two shares—his and sister Vida's. This gives me three shares—Duke's, Vida's, and mine. Now I barter with Mama to buy her share—give her the money but let her keep it until her death! And give her a home until her death. Then it would be mine. This now gives me four shares–232 acres! A home for my family, and my mother.

My brother Duke and Ethell's Dad Lonnie bond together to put a new roof on the old ancestral home, and a new screened porch around the side and front of the house. My very dear friend Julian McQueen, a carpenter's son and now a very good carpenter in his own right, agrees to do major changes inside the old house with Ethell's help. She is the architect, and he is the carpenter. They do a complete make-over. Everywhere there's a window, they put a door. Everywhere there is a door, they put a window. None of the doors and windows were the same height, so they proceeded to level them. You could see the chickens under the house through the big cracks in the floor, so they proceeded to re-floor the house. Tile where it belonged–beautiful oak hardwood floor where it belonged. Wall-to-wall carpet where it belonged. And, Oh, Yes! A new, and complete, bathroom with tub and shower, tiled floors, closets, the whole works. The old floors were made out of 5/4" x 6" heart, fat-lightard (lightwood) pine. You could not sand them, so we floored over the top of them. They put a bedroom where the parlor (living room) was. They put the living room where the family (master) bedroom was. They made a dining room out of a bedroom. They made a den out of the old dining room. They made a kitchen big as a mule pen. Ha! No kidding! You could almost live in the thing. Upper and lower cabinets around the walls; and a BIG pantry (a storeroom which accommodated a 20-ft. deep-freezer, washing machine, dryer, utility/broom closet–you name it–we had a place for it all). Plus, the stove, the kitchen sink, two refrigerators, and a big kitchen table, and chairs. We cooked, ate, worked, and played in the thing.

Ethell cooking in the old kitchen

Ethell and I then decided it was time to take care of Mama. We built her a little apartment. She had access to the bathroom, which joined her bedroom, a little breakfast room, and a cute, neat, cozy, multiwindowed sunroom on the east side of the house—all built on as an addition to the main house. Mama could now be with us any time she wanted to, but she could also go to her little apartment and be all alone any time she wanted to. And still be secure. And never leave the house. This made her very happy. She seemed to be quite contented. And so were we.

Ethell and Julian had done a superb job of making a complete hallway from the front porch into the living room down the middle of the house into the back bathroom. The original hall was so wide that this was possible even after adding a new bathroom on the left side of the hall. They also created an upstairs by putting in a half bathroom and two bedrooms, in addition to making a huge attic storeroom with the remaining space. This upstairs bedrooms and storeroom was originally the large attic of the house.

Julian McQueen became very dear to us. More like a son than a hired worker. He ate with us any time he wanted to. He carried milk and butter home with him any time, any amount he wanted. There was no finer man around. He is still REAL special to us today. (More about him later.)

We figure the old house is now about 200 years old. It was originally built in two sections. The main section was four rooms—three bedrooms and a living room, with a kitchen and dining room built together, but separated from the main house with a covered walkway joining them. This was in case there was a fire in the kitchen, the whole house would not burn. Hopefully. Everything was heated with wood. The wood-heated cook stove had a water reservoir attached to the side to provide hot water for the household. And a warming closet was attached on the back of and above the main stove. This was to put the cooked food in to keep it warm until served. The house was heated by wood in a fireplace in the chimney. You were heated in the bedroom with flannel sheets, wool blankets, and feather bedspread or comforter. This top cover was over a cotton mattress covered with a feather mattress. You were covered with long-handled wool underwear. The long-handles had sleeves down to the wrists, and legs down to the ankles, with a flapped back door (trap door) for "special purposes".

Keeping wood cut from the forest and hauled to the house for the stove (stove-wood) and the house (house-wood) was quite a chore. The stove-wood was cut into small pieces to put in the small fire box of the stove, while the house-wood was cut into large pieces to fit into the fireplace in the chimney. The wood was cut in large quantities and stacked to dry or cure at the wood pile. The trees were felled by a cross-cut saw about six feet long with a handle on each end and pulled back and forth by two men on opposite sides of the tree. The felled trees were then cut into blocks the length of your stove box and the width of your fireplace. The blocks were then split with a four pound axe on a three foot handle into the size you used in the house for the stove and fireplace. You toted (carried) enough wood into the house to last all night or through a rain to keep it dry so it would burn. The small kids could bring in the wood in their little red wagon. This toy, the little red wagon, was used for many chores as well as for fun, especially pulling the baby, and everything else you could imagine.

I forgot to tell you that after Daddy died in 1921, the family built an addition onto the house. They built a dining room and kitchen and back bedroom onto the back of the house and removed the old unattached ones. They sank a hand pitcher pump just outside the new kitchen door, so Mama would not have to tote water in the cold, bad weather from the yard or the well.

Vision with me, if you will, where we started from to where we are now. The original four-room house (three bedrooms, one living room/parlor, with dining room and kitchen attached by covered arched walkway, to a modern (for that time-frame), seven room country home (four bedrooms, one living room, dining room, and kitchen) all in one unit. The home was originally heated with wood in open fireplaces; the cooking was done with wood; there was no running water; and the toilet was an outside outhouse with one or two holes in a wooden seat (adult and child). Sears Roebuck catalogues and corn cobs were the accessories. Bath water was heated on the wooden cook stove or in the sunshine. You bathed in the back yard in three-bushel tin tubs. There was no running water. There was no electricity.

NOW: We live in a very modern, attractive, country estate home. With all the modern conveniences, fixtures, utilities—everything from necessities to luxuries. Special thanks to my Senator, and friend, Strom Thurmond, who got electricity run to my house out in the country. This was indeed quite a SPECIAL FAVOR at that time. Also, thanks again to my aforementioned friend, Julian McQueen and his very SPECIAL assistant, my precious, talented wife Ethell. She told Julian what she wanted, and they did it. The final addition was an eight foot broken tile screened-in porch across the entire front of the house around the corner and down the main side of the house to the new kitchen—about seventy feet—with entrances from the front and side and kitchen doors. A two-car carport was also added, along with two dormers on the front roof.

Newton Home, 1959

Newton Home, after remodeling, 1984

My State Senator then got the road in front of our house paved and called it Newton Road. My County Commissioner cut a road through my farm for me and called it Plantation Road. We installed a six inch deep well electric pump and dug us a farm pond. We are working hard and having fun.

Agriculture was also very interesting to me since I was a farm boy. While enrolled in Agriculture, I became a proud member of the FFA–Future Farmers of America. This served me well while growing up on the farm. It probably had some influence on me also. When I returned from overseas, and was retired from the Army, I came back to the family farm and enlisted in the Farm Program offered by the government to young farmers in order that they might become established in farming. While in this program, I assisted the director of the program in McColl, South Carolina, in starting the YFA (Young Farmers of America). We presented our program to the State authorities and started the South Carolina Association of the the YFA. I was elected the first Vice President. Kester Bodie was elected the first President. He was closer to Columbia, and much more available to assist in starting the state organization. I became the organization's second President. I was very active in assisting to get this organization started state-wide by counties; and then we proudly watched and helped it go nationwide. The National Young Farmers Association. It was my pride and joy. I remained active until I was to old to be active. I was then, and still am, an honorary member of the State and National organizations. I am quite proud to have started, and to be a member of this fine organization.

Jack (2nd from the right) on cover of Y.F.A. publication,
September 1950

I have been appointed school Trustee, Sunday School teacher, Church Lay Leader, Charge Lay Leader, and District Associate Lay Leader of the Church. I am a very active Lay Speaker. I helped organize the Young Adult Fellowship. I am in the Farm Bureau. I am in The American Legion, The Veterans of Foreign Wars, and The Reserve Officer Association. I am a Retired Lt. Col. in the United States Army. I was the first State Vice President of the Y.F.A., and the second President. All of this, in addition to my farming operations. I guess you would say I was an undercover politician.

Well, again, I have gotten all involved in my home preparation and repair and other organizational activities and have neglected to keep you abreast of my family reproduction and my family activities. However, I can assure you that nothing that I have constructed or planted in the last eighteen months can match the handiwork that my productive precious wife has accomplished. For the fifth time, I get this urgent message from My Darling—each one the same as the first. "I must go! And

NOW!" And so, we went! To the Marlboro County Hospital in Bennettsville, South Carolina, on May 14, 1949, where she produced a full-grown (over nine pounds) precious baby boy from a tiny seed I had planted nine months ago. What a miracle. We named him Donald Andrew Newton (D.A.N.). Now PETER has a brother ANDREW. What a pair they have been. What a pair they are. "Don" must prove his value, however. He only cost half as much as Pete! He only cost us $150.00 to get him from the hospital. What a BARGAIN! We've been proud of our shopping spree ever since. They are all five of EQUAL value. Three Queens and a Pair of Jacks make a FULL HOUSE. You know they are a True Winner. I surely hope all of my farm plantings will be so valuable. They have all grown in favor with God and Man. This completes my earthly family. God said, Be fruitful and multiply. Again, how He has Blessed this Man. There are now fifty-three of us! Five children, their spouses (five), grandchildren (eleven), their spouses (nine), great-grandchildren (seventeen, plus another one due this year), step-grandchildren (one), and spouse (one) great-grand step-child (one), me, (Ethell), and now Murl (story forthcoming) equals fifty-three.

By the time Don is born, I have two little girls in school. Lynn and Ronna. What a pair! Of course, Lynn is one grade ahead of Ronna. Pete is in line just one and a half years behind. Now Tricia and Don are our babies.

I cannot proceed further without devoting space to some of the activities and events of my precious, sweet, adorable, wife Ethell—my helpmate. I guess I must start with quite an honor that was bestowed upon her—Master Farm Homemaker of South Carolina. She eventually served as President of the South Carolina M.F.H. Association, and as Secretary of the National Master Farm Homemakers Association. Through her association with this organization, we both were able to travel to a number of different states and acquire many wonderful friendships. With all of her work on the farm, her remodeling of our 200-year-old home, her work with and for, and her devotion to her church, her children's school activities, her community activities, her care-taking of an aging mother-in-law, her being the perfect help-mate for her farming, war veteran husband with his wounded right hand, his ulcerated stomach, and anxiety reaction complex, and finally and most importantly, being the most wonderful Mother of our five children, the honor seemed quite appropriate and was deeply appreciated. It was quite an honor for her to become a Master Farm Homemaker. She is certainly that, and so much more.

Ethell, Jack, holding Don, Lynn, Ronna, Pete, Pat (front left)

Everybody loves her so much. And she loves everybody, too. She is so sweet, so friendly, so natural, so much at ease. On this basis, she is asked to be the Welcome Wagon hostess for Marlboro County, and she accepts. Again, everybody loves her.

She is also President of the local W.O.W. (Woodmen of The World) lodge. In addition, she becomes the Hostess for McDougald Funeral Home in Laurinburg, North Carolina, and dearly loves it, and EVERYBODY loves her.

Most of all, she is my Precious Wife, and the Mother of our children. She is Quite A Lady and has always been My Lovely Lady.

CHAPTER 14

I now own four-fifths of my dad's South Carolina estate, as stated earlier. I am deeply involved in bringing it into full production. What a challenge! First, because I am my daddy's Farm Boy. Second, I am an educated Chemist. I am God's Boy. I want to take what God has provided in nature and use what He has permitted me to achieve through education and talent which He gave me through birth, and the ambition and desire with which He has endowed me, to use to the extent of my ability to produce the maximum yield and top quality attainable. At the same time, I want to preserve, maintain, and if possible, to improve the land that He has entrusted me with. I am proud of who I am. I thank God for His blessings. And pray to Him–Oh! So often–to guide me in my efforts to provide for my own household and to be an asset instead of a liability to my family, my friends, and my community. I thank Him again, and again, and again for my beautiful, wonderful wife.

First, as a chemist, I must find out what I have to work with. Then what I am going to do with it. How I will get maximum results. How I will develop the finest, top quality products. To do this–I must determine what assets I have from all sources. And then to use them wisely, and to the best of my knowledge and ability. God has provided the base–the land. I must plant the highest yielding–best grade varieties. I must fertilize with the proper plant food elements for the particular crop I am planting. I must apply the maximum amount of this fertilizer that the plants will consume to produce the maximum yield without waste. I must be economical. I must plant high germinating seed. I must control the insects with the best insecticides using the proper amount at the proper time. I must know when to start and when to stop planting, fertilizing, spraying, and harvesting. I must be thorough. But I must be economical. I must control the undesirable vegetative growth with the best chemical and manual effort. I must harvest in a timely, most efficient manner. I must have the highest yield and the best quality. I must be especially careful of the moisture content at harvest, and the efficiency of the harvesting equipment. I must be economical. But also, I must be productive. Then I must be wise in marketing, and frugal in handling my finances.

To accomplish the above requirements, I must test the soil in each field. I take small samples of soil from all over the field, mix them thoroughly, then take a composite sample from the mixed samples and number the sample to match the field from which it came. I do this for each field on my farm. I then send them to a special Soil Testing Laboratory to determine what plant food elements are in the soil. I then determine which of, and the amount of, these elements that the crop to be planted will consume during the growing season. I then apply the maximum quantity of that specific analysis of fertilizer, plus a little, to the soil before I plant the crop to assure maximum yield.

Your first soil sample analysis will tell you if the food elements in your soil are: VP, P, M, H, VH (Very Poor, Poor, Medium, High, Very High). You now add the proper food elements, in the proper amounts, to give you a medium analysis on all of your plant food requirements. You annually replace all food elements to maintain a medium analysis—plus the amount of the desired mixed fertilizer to feed the crop that you are going to plant. You now know the crop you are going to plant; the analysis (kind) of fertilizer that your crop will consume (eat) and the amount that it will eat. You need to apply this amount of this analysis to the soil for maximum production. This is EDUCATION. This is CHEMISTRY. This is ECONOMY.

You get the most and the best for the least.

Feeding cotton and tobacco is kind of like feeding a horse and a baby. You feed each his own required food, and the required amount—with the least waste. Each plant eats its own kind and amount of food. This is what you feed it. The most nourishment with the least waste yields the most profit.

Fertilizer put into the ground that is not consumed is a waste. Profit, and Care and Maintenance of the soil, is the bottom line.

To continue along this line, you use the highest quality seed of the highest yielding variety, and the right amount to give you the right amount of plants per acre to produce the highest yield per acre to produce the highest profit per acre. You send your seeds off to have them tested for percent germination and treated for disease. This tells you how many plants per foot of row you will have and treats the young plants for soilborne disease and sucking insects. You treat the soil with a chemical to prevent other soilborne diseases and undesirable weeds and grasses. This gives your plants a healthy start. You cultivate, add fertilizer, and apply insecticides as needed until harvest. You now make sure that your harvesting equipment is mechanically at its best. You seek to accomplish the most efficient harvest with the least possible waste! This is EDUCATION. This is CHEMISTRY. This is THE BOTTOM LINE.

Again, you must be wise in your marketing of your crop. You have done your homework. You have been a good steward of the soil. You have applied all of your education in chemistry and mechanics. You have used your God-given talent–all to the best of your knowledge and ability. You must not goof off now. You must use all the information and contacts available.

Now for the real bottom line: How do you handle your finances? Your NEEDS must be met. Your expenses must be paid. BUT. . .BEWARE of credit. You can almost live off of the high interest of a large debt. Do Not borrow a dollar that you do not need. My advice is, "If you can't pay for it, don't buy it!" I have followed this policy all of my life. You must be FRUGAL. I'll leave the rest of this story to the proper sources.

The above practices I tried to put into effect from the first day I started farming. (1) I tested the soil. (2) I treated the seed. (3) I applied the fertilizer. (4) I planted the variety. (5) I applied the proper pesticides, herbicides, and insecticides to the soil and to the growing plants. (6) I controlled the undesirable weeds and grasses. (7) I did a timely harvest. (8) I used the markets to my best advantage. (9) I never borrowed money that I did not need. (10) I used my finances to the best of my educated, God-given ability. I was a Successful Farmer.

Jack on the tractor

I purchased two of the farms joining me. I remodeled my home twice. I educated my five children. I did all of this with the 100% help and TLC (Tender Loving Care) of my precious, wonderful, loving, understanding wife, Ethell. Without her, her understanding, her encouraging, her patient and support-ing efforts, I would have been just another pronoun. To have her, the mother of our five children, was one of God's blessings to this man and our five children! She, and the children did the home and barn chores, and then worked on the farm, in the fields, when needed, and as time permitted. They were ex-cellent help–pulling weeds, picking cotton, puttin' in tobacco, grading and preparing the crop for market, harvesting potatoes, canning garden produce (corn, beans, peas, tomatoes, grapes, etc.). They were The BEST! Never had any trouble with any of them! Note: Still don't have any. Their SNOOP PATROL is too good! They keep each other well informed. Can you imagine how proud this eighty-nine-year-old Farm Boy is?

Jack with his tomatoes

This story would not be complete without a few of my special projects. (It will never be complete anyway! Ha! Ha! You didn't really expect me to tell EVERYTHING, did you?)

Early in my farming days, I bought twenty sheep: nineteen Ewes (females), and one Ram (male). I eventually had a herd of forty. They came from Montana. This is something I had never heard of in my section of the country. I thoroughly enjoyed the project. It was also profitable. I sold the wool and the mutton (meat).

I also ventured slowly into the Hereford Cattle business. I bought ten cows (female) and one bull (male). This project I really developed. The Registered cattle came from a Wyoming Hereford Ranch. The little bull that I bought was eighteen months old and cost me $750.00. His full brother (same Mother–same Daddy) was purchased, I am told, for $112,000.00. My bull, BACA DUKE was bred in Pulaski, Tennessee. He was the main attraction at an auction and was held until the last to hold the buyers. Time ran out for the buyers to stay any longer and still catch their planes, so at the end of the sale, most all of the buyers were gone or had already bought. Hence, I got my prize almost as a gift. He grew, and developed into, one of the finest, most beautiful, specimen of any Hereford bulls that I have ever seen until this day. I kept him until old age. My herd finally increased to 105. I finally sold all of the herd. And I went entirely to row crop farming.

I also had purchased a black, five-gated saddle mare with a white crescent in her forehead. She was truly my pride and joy! She was named Black Beauty–and a beauty she really was. There was nothing like her in my area. She was mine, Ethell's, and the children's. But especially Pete's and Don's. I could write a book on Black Beauty and The Boys. We also raised a fine specimen of our own. We named this horse, Blaze. He, too, became part of the family. This type of farming and activity really kept Pete and Don engaged. They grew to be EXPERTS at any part of it. I could trust them implicitly, whatever the task. The five of them were really Three Queens and a Pair of Jacks—a Full House—a winning hand. With their Mother Ethell, Daddy Peter Jack, and their Granny Newton, it was also a House Full. We were really a close-knit group. With the eventual forming of The Snoop Patrol, we are still very close today. We have since added Murl and her family, after Ethell's and Mac's (Murl's husband) deaths. How the Good Lord has blessed us! The Snoop Patrol keeps everybody informed and up to date. My family is My Life! What I was—was for them. What I am truly is because of them. I could write about them—each one individually and as a family group for the rest of my life. Again, I say, they have been and are my life. What a wonderful life! Almost Heaven on Earth. What more can you ask? How blessed can you be? I am so-o-o happy! I am so satisfied. I am so contented. Again, and again, and again—I thank God for all of His blessings.

CHAPTER 15

Back to the farm: Almost everything has changed. As I stated above, I have gone entirely to Row Crop farming, and grain. I have bought a tractor, planters, cultivators, sprayer, and a combine; a truck, a cotton-picker, and other necessary accessories. The mule, and horse & buggy, and hand-plows are GONE. The hand-picking of cotton, the reap and binder, and thrasher for grain are GONE. The cotton is picked by hand no more. Everything is mechanical. Marketing has even gone modern. So, have banking and finances. Even schools and family lifestyle. Social life and ethical standards have drastically changed. Computers, cell phones, transportation, and just about every other aspect of life–even war–have changed. All of the above have drastically affected my life. But God does not change. We are born, we live, and we die. I will leave the rest of this to theologians, historians, politicians, chemists, scientists, educators, and morticians.

My family practices and efforts based on education, chemistry, determination and persistence did not go in vain or unnoticed. I had been farming only about five years when my yield and my quality really were paying terrific dividends. I was harvesting one and one-half to two bales of cotton per acre when other farmers were harvesting only one-half of one bale per acre. I was winning in the county contests. I was harvesting 199 bushels of corn per acre compared to thirty - forty bushels per acre harvested by others. I had similar results with grain and soybeans. Education and chemistry were paying off.

Jack in cotton field

Jack overseeing Irrigation pipelines

I had converted a mule-drawn insect-duster to a tractor-mounted duster at the local machine shop. This caused much speculation and conversation. My practices and my activity seemed enough to have me committed. My education and my chemical practices seemed somewhat out of line. BUT when I harvested my crops, and my yield was so much more than others, they wanted to know what I had done and how I had done it.

One of the greatest things that ever happened to farming in my time was the High-Boy self-propelled sprayer. All we had before were the dusters and the walk-behind sprayer. Needless to say, the effectiveness of the duster depended so much on the weather conditions. If there was a strong wind, it blew all the dust away—and your money, too. You had to dust at night and early morning while the dew was on the plants to catch and hold the dust. If there was no dew, your effort was wasted—and so was your money. The time frame to do the job was very limited; whereas the sprayer mist provided its own moisture and could be applied twenty-four hours per day. What a difference in the effectiveness of the poison, the precision of the timing, and the yield of the crop.

Where does this come into my life? I owned and operated the ONLY Hahn High-Boy self-propelled sprayer in our entire region. I bought it from the supplier out west. It was brought from Indiana behind a pickup truck. It was a tricycle type, tubular framed structure, driven by a Wisconsin motor. It had a top-mounted seat with a steering wheel up through the frame. Its tank was under-slung, and the spray rig was behind. It was a sight to see. And it was extremely efficient. The boll weevil and the lice died almost instantly when sprayed with the High Boy compared to dusting. It was almost like a miraculous breakthrough in farming. They brought it here with the front wheel mounted in the pickup truck and the two rear wheels trailing behind. I had a few changes made at the local machine shop to suit my specifications and put it to work.

Needless to say, we (my sprayer and I) were the talk of the entire countryside. At harvest time, my cotton fields were white and like no other. My yield was unbelievable. People came from near and far to see the snow-white fields. Some would stop and chat after making pictures. Many contracted with me to custom spray their crops for them the following year for so much per acre. After the second year, I had more requests for custom spraying in both South and North Carolina than I could possibly handle—even working every day for twenty-four hours per day. Some area farmers had the local machine shop make copies of my machine for them. My business and my machine lasted for years.

I guess the most disastrous event in my farm life was the warehouse fire. I had built the best farm warehouse, with shelters on both sides and the rear. A farm-machinery shed, if you will, to best protect my investments. It was to house and to hold my valuable farm equipment—tractors, planters, harvesters, sprayers, etc.

One particular day, I had provided a tractor, with equipment, to assist my crippled brother, Raleigh. He had provided the driver, a local farm hand, to help him get planted. At the end of the working day, the driver brought the tractor and equipment home and properly stored it under the shed. But before he left the shed, he proceeded to steal some gas from the tractor. In doing so, he spilled some of the gas. Even worse, he was smoking. He proceeded to discard what he thought to be a snuffed cigarette butt; however, it still had fire on its tip. Instantaneously, the stored hay and cotton, the building, the machinery, and the pick-up truck, all went up in flames. I was destroyed. So, everyone thought. I had four kids in college. And I had debts that are normal to farm and crop production.

I think every merchant and dealer that I owed—except one—had an agent in my yard within forty-eight hours to collect their bill. They all figured with such a tremendous loss—everything I had—that my farming days were over. Each one figured he would be first to get his share of what I had left. Almost no one farming had insurance during those days. I had none, except on my house.

The exceptional one was Mr. Edwin Pate of Z. V. Pate, Inc. Instead of sending an agent, he placed a personal phone call requesting that I come to his office just as soon as possible. He was just as nice and sympathetic and understanding as he possibly could have been. I had bought most all of my tractors and equipment from him. I owed him more than I did anyone else.

My opinion of friends, business partners, merchants, and associates, was at a pretty low ebb, to say the least. Really at rock bottom. How could they be so cruel? Did I have a surprising answer for them. As each agent expressed his sympathy and presented his bill, I presented him with a check Paid in Full, and wished him well in their future business. You see, the Good Lord had been so good to me, and blessed me so well, that I had made a profit EVERY year I had farmed, except one. That year, an early summer hail literally destroyed my entire cotton crop. But I managed. Remember, I had survived the depression.

The Good Lord had blessed me with a wonderful mother, a wonderful wife, and five wonderful children. I had been taught that credit would destroy you; and that you should save for a rainy day; that there was as much in saving as there was in making; that a penny saved is a penny earned; and honesty is the best policy. Remember, I had lost my daddy when I was four years old, and I was the baby of fourteen. I had been taught all of the above; and for fear of what could happen again that had happened in the past, I had literally saved every penny, every nickel, every dime, yes—every dollar—that I did not have to spend for survival. This amount for a farmer was indeed quite a bit. Enough that I was able to pay off all of the above creditors, except the one exception, Mr. Edwin Pate.

This is another story! I honored Mr. Pate's phone call and went to see him within the forty-eight hours. He invited me in and made me feel "at home". At least "at ease". He was truly sincere in his concern for my loss. He began by telling me that his father and my father had been great friends and business partners; and that he and I, he believed, were just as involved with each other and concerned for each other as our fathers had been, if not more so. Now he would not take any more of my busy time, but please do him a favor. Go around to the tractor and equipment shop and tell them that he said, "Replace all that I had lost and put me back in business just like I was before the fire." With tearful thanks, I started out the door when he called to me, "Oh! Peter Jack, have them up-date it a little. Some of it is getting a little old!" Not a word about the debt! Needless to say, this was one of the experiences of my life. He was always "Paid in Full". What an influence so many people have had on this Country Boy's life!

Life goes on, and years go by. You would think by now that we have long settled down. We have—so far as is possible—but, "There is nothing so constant as change". Farming practices, machinery, finances, mechanization, etc.; mules and plows, harvesting, shucking corn by hand, picking cotton by hand, family milk cows, killing hogs, and share cropping are over! Gone! And so is the general family "lifestyle". The whole world has changed. Yes, my family has changed along with the times. It is now tractors, planters, chemicals, sprayers, combines, and cotton pickers; cars, cell phones, planes, and cruise ships!

I do not dare pursue this train of thought and actions any further here. There are libraries and museums full of such material!

CHAPTER 16

My Beautiful Bride and I celebrated our twenty-fifth anniversary with a spur of the moment trip with my brother Duke and his wife, Lib. As previously stated, Duke and Lib, and Ethell and I were married on the same day, and at the same time, but 100 miles apart. We always called to wish each other "Happy Anniversary"; but on the eve of our twenty-fifth, Ethell and I took off to Columbia to Duke's house. They didn't know we were coming. The next morning, with no plans, the four of us took off to Pensacola, Florida, to see our sister Lucille and her husband Bob. And quite a trip it was! Duke was always a prankster, and he hadn't changed a bit. And his junk had rubbed off on me over the years, too. Being our Second Honeymoon, suffice it to say, we had a ball!

How life changes! It seems almost like yesterday that I was a college student. Today I am the Dad of college students. Lynn and Ronna, the two older girls, have made their choices of colleges to attend. Now it's Pete's turn, but not quite so simple. You would surely think that Dad would send his son to Wofford, and rightly so; But, sometimes circumstances demand change. I can't overlook the world situation. I cannot forget my military life and its consequences. You can get an education at many colleges, but some have better military preparation, such as outstanding R.O.T.C. I could not help but think "What if. . ." as in my past. My sons should be prepared the best possible for the worst possible. Then hope and pray that it never comes. It was with this bearing heavily on my mind that Dad helped Pete decide to go to Clemson.

You see, Clemson had an Air Force R.O.T.C. Wofford only had Infantry. In the Air Force, you were always in the air, or on home base. Hot food, fresh food, warm dry bedding; the most possible safety in the rear areas, riding all the time, and actual combat only when you were in the air, except bombings, raids, etc. In contrast, when in the Infantry and in actual combat, you had "C" Rations—food in cans—that you carried on your backs; a bed roll, wet or dry, hot or cold, depending on the weather, that you carried on your back; a heavy rifle and ammunition that you carried on your back; a heavy, uncomfortable steel helmet that you wore on your head; heavy combat boots that you wore on your tired, aching, frozen feet in the mud, in the snow, in the water; and you walked most all of the time. And you had to be combat ready for attack or defense, from the air, from the ground, from the sea twenty-four hours of every day. Every tick of the clock. It could be bombings, or strafing bullets from the air; shelling by artillery from a distance; shelling by mortars and tanks at close range; machine gun fire, and rifle fire within eyesight, and hand-to-hand fighting, eyeball to eyeball. You walked, ate, slept, and fought in the rain, in the mud, in the snow, and in the hot sun. You had a slit-trench dugout in the ground for a latrine or toilet. You doctored your wounded on the battlefield and carried them by hand to the rear. The dead were cared for by a special unit. Hearing the screaming wounded, watching the shattered bodies blown apart limb by limb, and faces and body parts all mangled up was too horrifying to describe. This was the Infantry. And this scenario was much more common on the ground than in some of the other branches of the service. These feelings, whether they be right or wrong, caused me to help my son Pete decide to go to Clemson and join the Air Force R.O.T.C. My son Don later got the same help, and also went to Clemson.

Pete graduated and was commissioned a 2nd Lt., U.S.A.F., and continued in the service for twenty-one years. He retired a Major. Don was also commissioned a 2nd Lt. in the U.S.A.F. when he graduated. He served his required time and left the service as a Captain. Pete was assigned to Mather Air Force Base in California and became an instructor. Don was assigned to Laredo Air Force Base in Texas, and he too became an instructor. They have both made Daddy and Mama mighty Proud! Of course, they both have their own stories to tell.

What a story I have to tell about Pete. During his service years, at one time he was stationed in Tai Chung, a short distance from Taipei in Taiwan—not far from China. He was there with his family at the time of our thirtieth anniversary. Ethell and I decided to go to see them. I could fly free Space A (space available) anywhere, anytime there was space available on the aircraft. If Ethell was with me, she could fly free, but only outside the USA. So, the plans are made. Ethell will fly commercial to Seattle, Washington. I will join her there by flying military aircraft free. We will then fly together on military aircraft to Alaska, and on to Taipei, free. This we did. We were treated like a King and Queen by the military. When we landed in Fairbanks, Alaska, there was a deep soft snow on the ground. I convinced Ethell that we should unload and literally walk in Alaska, so we could tell all our friends that we had been in Alaska. Just as she departed from the plane to the snow-covered ground, and being the gentleman that I was, I was (supposedly) helping her not to fall; but being the Little Devil that I was, I (intentionally) tripped her and fell into her, knocking her down in that pretty white snow. As she fell, I did all that I could to help completely bury her in the snow, and then fall on top of her. What a ball we were having! This was just the beginning.

We arrived at Taipei about two o'clock in the morning. How will we get to Tai Chung? I convinced the authorities to help with our plight—us in Taipei at two o'clock in the morning and our son in Tai Chung. They finally agreed to send us to Tai Chung on a military C-130. Can you believe it? It was so wonderful to get Ethell a flight on a military C-130. "A thirtieth anniversary present," they told Ethell. It seemed to us that they were flying about house-top level. I was so excited.And I don't remember how we actually got from Tai Chung to Pete's house.

We are now at Pete's and Libby's. What a ball we are to have. Libby was really quite a hostess. Pete had arranged for us to go out our anniversary night. They carried us out to a Big Ball—Guy Lombardo style! The ushers told us there was no room except right on the front row—right in front of the orchestra pit. What dignitaries! We just didn't know. We soon found out. There was dinner, and dancing—the works. The orchestra played a very special song for very special guests on their thirtieth anniversary, "You Are My Sunshine", for Col. and Mrs. Peter Jack Newton, requested by their son, Major & Mrs. Peter Jack Newton, Jr. And on it went. Pete had arranged the whole thing.

One quick side not about another visit with Pete. While he was stationed at Mather AFB in Sacramento, California in 1971, I visited him for the birth of my granddaughter, Tara. Since San Francisco was nearby, I took a quick excursion to see what all the hippy commotion was about. It was one of the most unbelievable sights I ever saw, and probably the most disturbing. I crossed the Golden Gate Bridge to Sausalito where they were having, or staging, this "Love-In" way of life. Their motto: "Make Love, Not War"—literally making love on the lawns, in the yards, right out in public. They believed in sharing everything. I followed one very prominent, very popular, very impressive girl as she visited around, from place to place and bar to bar. She was evidently very rich. She treated the visitors, paid their bills, and seemed to be everybody's friend.

That was the idea—one for all and all for one. Everybody loved everybody. I just was not used to that—especially the public lovemaking!

On our way home, we decided to come a different direction. We came back to the states to Travis Air Force Base in California. From there, Ethell caught her commercial flight home. I continued my Space A, but I had a surprise waiting for me. Our plane developed engine trouble and went down in Altus, Oklahoma. I knew why they called it Altus. That plane went down, and Alt-us went down with it. And Alt-us were the only ones there. It was Thanksgiving holidays, and everything was closed except for a skeleton crew. Just the opposite was happening at my home in South Carolina. All of my family were gathering for the Thanksgiving holidays. Ethell had arrived home, and she and the family had a blowout, including Welcome Home greetings, etc. But where was Daddy? No one knew. He was in Altus, Oklahoma, almost all alone. No crew to repair the motor, but really thankful that all was well with the plane, the crew, and the passengers. When the plane was ready, we were off for home. There were no more difficulties. I was several days late arriving home, but glad to be home safe.

Ethell and I have continued living at The Old Home Place. No two people anywhere could be happier, more satisfied, more contented, or more THANKFUL to Almighty God than we are. We are active in community life, in church activities, and in business. But change must come.

In 1983, just before planting time, an aggressive young farmer comes to see me with a proposition. He wants to rent my land. He informs me that he knows what it would take per acre to rent it, but that he can't afford that. My answer was jokingly, "Not one penny less!" My farm was really not for rent. He left with the request that if I ever decided to rent,

PLEASE give him first choice. He said that he could make more profit from one acre of my land at that price than he could make on an acre free from the land he was presently renting. He left asking me not to forget him.

He returned ten days later with a check in his hand and a smile on his face telling me that he was going to rent my land, and that I would be proud of his work. I was flabbergasted. My land was not for rent. He insisted that I had told him to the penny, and he had borrowed the money. I could not back out.

I can't believe it until this day, but I rented him my land! I was sixty-seven years old, and all of my family was gone. What would happen if I got sick, or had an accident, or even worse? What a burden would be on Ethell. Again, no land rent was higher—but no land was better, more productive, tiled for drainage, and soil tested for maximum production. It was still a good deal for the young man. It is still top quality, maximum productive land today. My present renter, Mr. T. G. Gibson, Jr., gives it first class attention—as if it were his own. He knows what it means to me.

With the land rented, I had no further use of all that farm equipment. It was to be a big step and a huge change in my life, but I immediately arranged for an auction sale. The equipment was in excellent condition, and I had an excellent sale. What a crowd.

Taking a break

I think my farming reputation definitely helped with my auction sale. So, did all of my five kids, and my wonderful wife. They were all ambassadors, and what an asset they were. With all of the pros, how could there be any cons? But there was one BIG one. A lifetime pride, possession, heritage was gone. So, it seemed. Of course, the entire farm was still there–with additions. And still is today. And will be there when I am gone! It is already divided among our children. To each his or her own share. Debt free.

This old man was now a Country Boy again. And with a world of experience behind me. College kid, professional chemist, army soldier, army officer, businessman, undercover politician, church man, school man, community man, family man, and now a proud, happy, quite successful Country Man (A matured Country Boy).

On the front porch

Ethell and I continued our lives for the next thirteen years, until her death–loving EVERY minute of it, together–with children, grandchildren, greatgrandchildren, friends, and extended families. She was all involved with our church, community, her Master Farm Homemakers Association, and Woodmen of the World. She was indeed Quite a Lady and loved by all who knew her.

One of Ethell's dearest friends that she grew up with, played basketball with, and courted with, became critically ill to the point of death. The doctors could not diagnose her illness, nor its cause. They advised her parents of their opinion, and together they shared the situation with Ethell's friend. She promptly told them that if Ethell knew this, she would come and pray with her, and that God would heal her. The parents called Ethell at our home 120 miles away and informed her of the situation and asked if she would come for the girl's comfort.

Ethell immediately mailed them a package containing an anointing cloth and asked them to place it on her friend's forehead and pray with her for God to heal her body and make her whole. She followed up with a phone call and was told that her friend was weaker. Whereupon Ethell hung up the phone, informed me that she was on her way to Georgetown, and was gone in no time. Upon arrival in the hospital, she questioned if they had followed her request. She was sheepishly told, "No." That was not a part of their practice. She requested the envelope containing the cloth, (which by chance they had not discarded), and they gave it to her. She immediately and lovingly placed it on her friend's forehead, and they prayed together. The friend dropped off to sleep, and Ethell bid them farewell, and proceeded on her way back home—120 miles. She had hardly gotten home when the phone rang. It was her girlfriend calling from her hospital bed, telling Ethell how much better she felt, and thanking her so much for coming. She said she felt wonderful and was ready to get out of bed.

This, she surely did. She was discharged from the hospital to go home a few days later. The friend continued to do well and lived for many years. You may interpret this story any way you please. We just thank God and give Him the Glory.

As for my family, we have survived, progressed with the change, and adjusted well. All five of the children finished their education. Two went to Clemson, one to Winthrop, one to The Medical College of South Carolina in Charleston, and one to Woman's College-UNC. All are now well-established. All are married and have families of their own. We are so PROUD of ALL of them. I could write a book about each of them.

Ethell & Jack with Chuck and Ronna, Pete and Libby, Lynn and Al, Pat and Don, and Pat and Gene

Our fiftieth anniversary was an occasion no couple could ever forget. On November 22nd, the date of our actual anniversary, I asked Ethell for a date, which she so graciously accepted, and out to dinner we went!

Our children and their spouses hosted a celebration to honor this milestone in our lives, and what a terrific job they did! A couple of nights before, they presented us with several wonderful mementos—one being a flag that had been flown over the U.S. Capitol in our honor. This was arranged and obtained for us by my friend, Sen. Strom Thurmond of South Carolina. Other mementos included a scrapbook of our fifty years together, a plate with a picture of Ethell and me which had been made for our twenty-fifth anniversary, and a framing of our original wedding announcement, together with the invitation to the fiftieth anniversary celebration. Then came the day of the big celebration, November 25, 1989. The children displayed the flag from the Capitol on the wall; and table items included photographs from our past, Ethell's original wedding shoes (which Pat modeled at one point during the festivities), and the scrapbook Lynn had put together. Music from The Big Band era played, and the cake was topped with a Hummel "50th Anniversary" figurine that Pete and Libby brought from Germany. We could not believe the mass of people who honored us. They came from all stages of our life. From far and near they came. Over 400 of them! There were family and relatives, high school and college buddies, army buddies, business and political connections, farmer friends and associates, Master Farm Homemaker friends, Young Farmer associates, Farm Bureau, Woodmen of the World, and church friends and officials. What a crowd. What an honor. My beautiful, lovely wife was right in the middle of it all.

And you know I was.

One of the most touching, the most memorable, the most soul-lifting experiences that I have ever had was when the life-size, lighted Cross was presented to old Boykin Church (now over 200 years old) in honor of (now in memory of) my beautiful, devoted, truly Christian wife, Ethell. It was dedicated to her on Easter Sunday, 2005, before her death in February 2006. It was hung on the wall above and behind the pulpit. It was hand-made by L. P. Rogers, Ethell's nephew, from one of the original old Boykin Church pews. The pews were constructed of heart pine, knot-free, and hand-finished on the seating and the back-resting sides. The vertical part of the Cross was made from the back section on the old pew, while the horizontal part was made from the seat. This presented the grain of the wood in the most beautiful display. It is lighted by an array of tiny bulbs recessed in the back of the Cross and spaced from the wall so that all you get is a beautiful halo glow. There is no bright and dim appearance—just the same beautiful glow throughout. I've never seen one quite like it.

Ethell and Jack at 50th Anniversary celebration

Cross Dedication for Ethell at old Boykin Church, 1995

Ethell & Jack, 1995

Now comes the tragedy of my life; the loss of my life; the loss of The Love of My Life. The loss of My Beautiful, Wonderful, Indescribable, Wife. My Lovely Lady. My Mate for fifty-six years.

She had to have the mitral valve in her heart replaced. Surgery was done in the Medical University of South Carolina (MUSC) in Charleston, SC. The surgery itself was quite successful as far as the replacement of the heart valve was concerned. However, the medication used in conjunction with the surgery caused the kidneys to dysfunction and destroy themselves. I was told by the doctors that this violent reaction by the kidneys to the drug was because Ethell had never taken any drugs in any quantity to cause her body to build up any immunity. Therefore, there was a battle between the kidneys' effort to defend the body and the invading drug. The kidneys lost and were turned into a pulp-like gel. This condition is what the kidney biopsy revealed. The only conclusion—there were no more kidneys—and death was certain.

My life ended also, as far as I was concerned, when my precious wife, Ethell, died on February 20, 1996. Her funeral was at old Boykin Church, the church of my ancestors. Burial was in Newton Cemetery, the burial grounds of my ancestors. It was one of the largest funerals I have ever attended.

What a tribute to my Lovely Lady. She wasn't just my better half—she was my better two thirds. Two of the songs we sang at her funeral live within ME and are a part of my very soul. "When we all get to Heaven, what a day of rejoicing that will be! When we all see Jesus, we'll sing and shout the victory!" is one. The other is "What a friend we have in Jesus! All our sins and grief to bear. What a privilege to carry EVERYTHING to God in prayer! Oh! What peace we often forfeit,

Oh! What needless pain we bear. All because we do not carry EVERYTHING to God in prayer!"

My final tribute to her is on her gravestone:

A BEAUTIFUL LADY

A DEVOTED WIFE

A WONDERFUL MOTHER

A CHILD OF GOD

Until then, My Darling!

GOD BE WITH YOU

'TIL WE MEET AGAIN!

Ethell R. Newton

CHAPTER 17

L ife goes on from day to day, and when at night I kneel
to pray, I thank God for my health, my family, and my
friends. They are all so nice to me. They make me feel
So Special. I truly thank Him for all the blessings He has bestowed on me. Then I assure Him that I am ready to go and
join Ethell, My precious wife, for fifty-six most wonderful
years. Please don't let me linger and be a burden on anyone.
I never thought I could be so LONESOME.

But, Oh! He has other plans for me that I never dreamed
of. Going about my daily routine sent me to Gibson, my little hometown, one day to get some free air in my portable
air tank at the filling station. At the same time, He sends a
wonderful lady to the same station to get gas in her sister's
car. She was born and grew up in the Gibson area in a prominent Gibson family about five miles north from my home.
Her aunts (Aunt Cora and Aunt Tiny), and her mother (Mrs.
Virginia), went to Boykin Church—my lifetime church—if you
remember. Her uncle lived across the highway passing my
home, about a half mile. She worked for Dr. Pate, our family
doctor in Gibson, and came to the Newton Reunion, so she
knew Ethell well. Her dad (Mr. Chris) farmed and worked in
the cotton gin when in season. She was Virginia Murl Gibson.
So, we were surely no strangers. She had married her high
school sweetheart. He also lived about five miles west from
me. We were all five miles from each other. She was working
for Dr. Pate, and her husband Eldred ("Mac") worked in the

drug store. He was Julian McQueen's brother. Remember Julian, my carpenter?

What a connection!

Shortly after Virginia Murl and Mac were married, they moved to Plymouth, North Carolina, after Mac had graduated from embalming school. (He had been employed by the local funeral home, and as mentioned above, Murl was employed by a local doctor.) Here is where they reared three children—Ginger (Virginia), Eldred, (Jr.), and Christy. They were well thought of and well respected. They were married forty-five years. Mac died in 1994. Their three children were all married. She was now living all alone. She owns and operates the Hillside Memorial Gardens Cemetery; and she has now retired from her work with Leggett Jewelry Store.

This wonderful lady, the same one that came to the gas station, now has her problem. Her sister, Chris, whose car she was putting gas into at the station, had had a stroke in 1995, and now can neither walk, nor talk. She is in a nursing home in Laurinburg, North Carolina (eight miles from Gibson). Murl takes turns with her sisters Emma Lee and Edna, taking care of her sister Chris, with the help of a Sitter. This is how she happened to be in Gibson, at the gas station—where I was—when I was.

While sitting in line waiting for service, she spotted me, and called to me. I went over. We asked about each other's health. She expressed her condolences about Ethell's passing. She told me about Mac's (Eldred's) passing, and her sister Chris's condition, and the reason for her periodic trips home to take care of Chris and staying at her Old Home Place with her sister Edna. She expressed her knowledge of my feelings without Ethell. After all she had just lost Mac about a year and a half earlier. At this time, the station attendant calls to Murl and informs her that if she does not move her car up, he is going to close the station and leave her sitting there. They are good friends.

A week goes by, and there is a funeral for a relative in Gibson. Would you believe? Yes, we are both there, and alone! She was so pretty, and very attractive. After the service she speaks to me, we chat a minute, but she must go. I tell her to give me a buzz sometime when she is back in town, and we will go out to eat. Away she goes. Until she stops as she is passing my next-door neighbor. You are right. There seems to be no time limit! I keep a casual glance in her direction until she leaves walking to her car. WOW! She looks as good going and she does coming! (I'm positive she knew I was watching) The next day, the phone rings. The voice on the other end: "Jack, this is Virginia Murl. I'm going home now, but when I get back, I'll give you a buzz, and we will go out to eat. Goodbye." The voice could not have sounded any sweeter. My entire body responded to it. I almost forgot my age. Anyway, I surely didn't feel eighty at this time!

What a change in my life had been wrought! Why now? Why her? After all, there were real nice widow ladies all around me. I had received phone calls. I had had visitors. The widow ladies in Ethell's Master Farm Homemakers Association were all exceptionally nice. Several had made it known that they were lonely and would like to be my mate. They loved Ethell so much. And thought that if she could love me like she did, they would be willing to take a chance. They really challenged me beyond expectation because they loved Ethell so much. One real nice lady, a multi-millionaire, challenged me to just leave all I had to the children and come to her, and that what was hers would be mine also. Ethell and I had visited her in her home. The home that I was looking for was in heaven, with my mate for fifty-six years. The Mother of our babies.

Back to my questions to myself: "Why now? Why her?" I truly believe that the Good Lord sent her to me. I do not question why her, nor the time. I just THANK Him for His most precious gift.

Sorry! I got ahead of myself. I haven't got her yet. But I am after her. Just follow me and the Good Lord. My daughter Lynn and her husband Al are visiting with me. She tells me that she and Al are going to see Aunt Agnes, in Belhaven, North Carolina. Aunt Agnes is Ethell's oldest sister. Lynn wants to know if I want to go. My whole body responds. But nobody knows why but me (and the Good Lord). Aunt Agnes and Belhaven are only twenty-seven miles from Plymouth. Murl lives in Plymouth! Are you with me? Or are you ahead of me? Al's and Lynn's new Cadillac is bound to be good for twenty-seven more miles—with or without them. My answer to Lynn is, "When are you leaving? Come pick me up!"

And we were off. We were well received by Agnes. We love her dearly. But I had not yet arrived at my planned destination. I call Al out to give him the news. He has two choices. One is to go with me. The other is I go alone in his Cadillac to Plymouth. He decides to drive me to Plymouth. What a trusting soul. We stop at a filling station when we get to Plymouth. I go in to get directions. He cleans his windshields. When we drive off, I jokingly inform him that they charged me $1.00 for him to clean the windshields. He has a fit. I tell him to calm down. They told me anybody that could afford a Cadillac could surely afford $1.00 to clean the windshields. As for my directions, I was within one mile of my destination. A left turn, a right turn, a left turn, a right turn, and I was there. We pull up in the yard and stop. I am out and gone to the door. Al's version: "This lady comes to the door with outstretched arms and just enfolds me into them. Then we disappear into the house. I'm gone for forty-five minutes before he sees me again." He still says, "That's my story, and I'm sticking to it." The lady is Virginia Murl. She tells Al we were "getting reacquainted." Al says, "Oh! That's what you call it?" Back to Agnes's we go. At least my body went. My mind was probably still in Plymouth. I tried to describe her to Al: "She is the prettiest, sweetest, cutest, most devilish thing you ever saw. In fact, she is down-right IRRESISTIBLE." Now, the longer I know her, the better that describes her! She is truly My Baby Doll.

We spend the night with Agnes, and head for Cape Hatteras, Nags Head, and The Outer Banks the next day. We take the ferry over to Ocracoke. Then another ferry to Cape Hatteras, Kitty Hawk, and Kill Devil Hills; but we drive around coming back. The last stop we make before we head for home is The Elizabethan Gardens in Manteo. Lynn checks the map for the route home. She tells Al that we take Hwy 64 through Plymouth to Raleigh. Plymouth is all I heard. I immediately sought an available phone and placed a call to. . .Plymouth . . .to Murl. . .to tell her to prepare the way; I'm coming through. But that I would stop in Plymouth long enough to carry her out to supper. Well, Excuse me. There is no answer. About half-way to Plymouth, I make another call—still no answer. Then, in Plymouth, we go by the house. No one is at home. We go to the restaurant for supper (really to kill time). While we were waiting to be served, I ask the waitress if I might use the phone. She says, "Sure." But it's behind the counter, behind the cash register. She will be glad to dial the number for me and hand me the receiver across the counter. She asked who I was calling, and the number. When I told her, she knew Murl real well, and told me so. She tried the number, but again—no answer.

She asked if she could help–give a message or tell her who was calling. I told her my name, our connection, and that she was a very dear friend. I proceed to have supper with Al and Lynn.

When we finish eating, the waitress comes over to give me the bill, sits down beside me, looks me dead in my eyes, tells me who she is, and very seriously explains her situation to me. She tells me that she and her husband have just separated, that she is now also considered a widow lady, and not to worry about Murl. If "I'm good enough for Murl–I'm good enough for her!" Just forget Murl. She will clock out and go with me right now. Just take her by her house to pack a bag. Too bad for Murl! She was not home! Well–I realize I am eighty years old, but I'm not quite ready for this. I thank the lady, pay the bill, and leave the lady standing at the door. I reluctantly agree to leave without seeing Murl but allow Lynn and Al to take me on home with them. (I found out later that the lady told Murl that I turned her down.)

Back home and lonely–but not for long. Murl calls me on the phone to tell me that she is in Greenville, North Carolina, with her daughter Christy to deliver her baby daughter Chelsea. She tells me that she will see me in Gibson (my home) real soon. And so, she does. And out to eat we go–to McDuff's! What a memorable occasion.

Quite a change in life is occurring. From Plymouth to Gibson, and back to Plymouth. Visits, phone calls, greeting cards, letters, poems, chocolates, and roses. This can't be for real. Murl's phone bill alone was over $100.00 one month. A lot of it was for prime time. When I reprimanded her for using prime time, she informs me that when she wants to talk to me, she will call me, "No matter what time of day or night it is." WOW! From then on, I answered the phone whenever it rang with pleasure.

My nights at Plymouth Inn were quite eventful. I must tell you about one of them. I had stayed with Murl until after midnight. I went to the Inn for the night and there was no vacancy. We called the other places. No vacancy. We called the adjoining towns. No vacancy. So, my friend at the Plymouth Inn had a suggestion: He would clean out a utility closet and put a roll-away bed in there for me. So, we did. Would you believe when I started to leave and went to tell my friend, "Thanks", he presented me with the bill–the same price as a regular room! I was really well-received in Plymouth. At least the utility closet was better than Murl did for me. She lived in her house all alone. THREE bedrooms! And she continued to live in her house ALL ALONE. Nothing new! That's what she and I were accustomed to–and in keeping with our parental training. She did let me move in after we were married.This was after a diamond bracelet for her birthday, a diamond watch for Christmas, a diamond engagement ring, and a wedding band. And a church wedding. We still had two extra bedrooms for invited guests.

I must not leave out the Dove Shoot. Every fall for the past eleven years, my sons Pete and Don invite our family, our friends, and our business associates to come and enjoy a Bar-B-Que dinner and Dove Shoot at the old family farm. Pete's wife Libby and Don's wife Pat help with the preparations, with Lynn, Ronna, and Sister Pat helping out with desserts, as it is a family affair to honor Daddy.

We especially invite some of Murl's people this year. Everybody gathers. The boys always ask Daddy to say a few words of welcome before we Thank the Good Lord for His Blessings. Bombshell! Daddy proceeds to PRESENT this SPECIAL, SPECIAL LADY that has become a very, very dear friend, as he holds Murl around her waist. What a surprise.

No one but the family knows about Murl at this time. She lives in Plymouth–200 miles away. Remember? What a shock wave hits the assembled crowd! This is September. We are married the following January.

CHAPTER 18

I must tell you about the trip to Hilton Head, South Carolina, as self-invited guests of my daughter Patricia (Pat) and her husband Gene. It was another one of those occasions of a lifetime. We arrive at beautiful Hilton Head and are escorted into this swanky condominium right on the waterfront—surely fit for a bridal suite. We eat at this swanky restaurant—surely fit for a reception. But, there has been no wedding, yet. But everyone seemed to know it was just a matter of time.

We wish Pat and Gene "Good night," and they return the wish for us. Gene especially wanted to emphasize the *good* night and *sweet* dreams. But none of them knew what was in store. Murl and I had gone out on the balcony quite excited with the beautiful full moon shining down on us and reflecting back on the calm rippling water. What a setting!

Add to this picture, a beautiful lady wrapped in my arms, with her eyes reflecting back in mine. Our hearts pounding away.

This old man was so excited, I was about to fall off the balcony. But I managed to slip my right hand into my pocket and bring out a beautiful diamond ring and slip it ever so gently on her pretty finger, place a kiss on her sweet lips and whisper to her to be my bride. After a lovely evening, we said "Good-night!"

The next morning, we told Pat and Gene. They were not too surprised. Gene goes to our room and comes back with the story that there was not but one bed with the covers really disturbed. I carried him back and showed him the wrinkled sheets on the other. Whereupon he immediately pulled out his shirt tail, twisted it up, and said, "I can do that, too!" as he proceeded to explain the wrinkled sheets on the second bed. We have a wonderful time, but before we part for home, sneaky Miss Pat has purchased a record for us, and in the proper setting, plays it for us. The main message is: "I may not love you for the rest of your life, but I'll guarantee you that I will love you for the rest of mine." Remember I'm almost eighty-one. Murl is sixty-five. What a record.

Well, if I am going to do all of this loving, I had better get married. The sooner, the better. She is My Baby Doll. I truly believe, I have no doubt, that the Good Lord has sent her to ME. I must love her, take care of her, cherish her, and keep her as long as I live. And help to provide for her as long as she lives, even after I am gone.

I tell her this, and she responds, "The wedding is on!" She is so pretty, so sweet, so cute, so devilish, and so, IRRESISTIBLE! The date is to be January 3, 1998, at her home church in Plymouth. Our very dear friend and Pastor Steve Creech will perform the ceremony.

The wedding is to be a family affair. Ten of hers, thirty-five of mine. She is a beautiful bride! The service is quite impressive and so is she. My son Don sings at the wedding. My daughter Lynn bakes the wedding cake. My son Pete and my daughter Pat have already endeared themselves. My daughter Ronna, now living at the Old Home Place, keeps the home fires burning and the good meals cooking. Murl's daughters Ginger and Christy busy themselves helping their Mother with the wedding plans and prepare dinner.

All went well.

Jack & Murl

After all weddings, there must be a Honeymoon! We had looked forward to this since Hilton Head. Lynn and Al come back into the picture and chauffeur us to Daytona Beach, Florida. What more can you ask? Everybody is so wonderful to us. Al accuses us of leaving footprints on the huge mirrored walls at the foot of our bed. I assure him that this is nothing unusual.

Mirrors have a tendency to reflect memories.

Life cannot be all roses. Storms are a part of nature. Lightning strikes. As I lay so peaceful with my head on Murl's heart with her sweetheart going *thump, thump, thump* in my ear, horrifying fear strikes! The sound changes to *thump. . .thump. . . thump. Thump, thump. Thump. . .thump. . .thump, thump, thump.* I think my precious wife is dying. Not now. Not here in Florida. "Please Lord. Please help me!" Murl refuses to permit me to call a doctor. She refuses to let me call home. "Just take me home," she cries!

I still don't believe it, but I let her prevail. I advise Al and Lynn, and we take off for home, several hundred miles away, with Murl in my arms in the back seat. Before we got there, it seemed like thousands. The Lord did what I asked. He helped me. We got her home and to the hospital. And we got her stabilized. She had Atrial Fibrillation. We got her sweet heart back into rhythm and on medication.

We had decided before we even married that we would make our home with Murl in Plymouth. As related earlier, I had retired from farming and rented the 400-acre farm to my doctor-friend, Dr. Gibson and his son, T.G. Gibson, Jr. T.G. still rents the farm today (2006). They couldn't take better care of it if they owned it. I am so satisfied—so pleased. In addition to my renting the farm, my daughter Ronna and her husband Chuck had come home to live with and to take care of me. I still have my little apartment there that I built on to the old home for my mother. Ronna and Chuck keep it neat, nice, and fresh for Murl and me, and feed us when we go home—which is quite often. It will be Ronna's when I die. The other four children will share the farm.

Now that Murl and I have settled into her home in Plymouth, I have come to love and be a part of her church family as well. Her Pastor Steve Creech and his wife have become my very dear friends, also. I would like to honor my beautiful new bride and her church (as I did my beautiful first bride) with a cross similar to the one dedicated to Ethell and hanging in old Boykin Church. Murl's daughters, Christy and Ginger and their families, and two of my children, Pete and Lynn and their spouses, were in attendance.

It was indeed a beautiful ceremony.

*Cross dedication for Murl at her church
in Plymouth, North Carolina*

Murl owns and operates the Hillside Memorial Gardens Cemetery in Plymouth. She owns, and lives in, her own home in Plymouth. She has a lovely home on Albemarle Sound, which is used by, and is for, the families. She and her husband Eldred (Mac) McQueen bought the property on the waterfront in 1959 and developed it. It is a beautiful place and extra special because they developed it. The terrible hurricane Isabel totally destroyed the building on 9/18/2003! She and I replaced it in April 2004. It is really nice. It is between Plymouth and Edenton. So instead of disrupting Murl's business, we decided to relocate me, since I was retired and could move my assets with me. It has been, and is, wonderful. We now live at Murl's home in Plymouth, at my home on the farm, or at our home on Albemarle Sound, as we so choose. But mostly at Murl's home.

Jack & Murl at their home on Albemarle Sound, NC

We make a point to be at Murl's on Mother's Day, Easter, and Christmas–for everybody. And at my place on Father's Day and Thanksgiving–for everybody. We celebrate our Newton Christmas on Thanksgiving. We celebrate our Clan Get-Together on the 4th of July at our Bateman Beach home on Albemarle Sound. The Clan consists of: The Peter Jack Newton and Ethell Rogers Newton clan, the Eldred (Mac) McQueen and Virginia Murl Gibson McQueen clan, and invited guests. We cook, eat, play in the water, lie in the sun, make home-made ice cream, shoot fireworks, and visit.

It would be hard for us to concede that there are any two people, anywhere, that are happier, more satisfied, more contented than we are. With God's continued blessings, and His will, so shall it continue to be.

This has been the life of this one Country Plowboy who grew up to retire from the U.S. Army as a Lieutenant Colonel. by the age of thirty. I have now come full circle and enjoy the life of being a retired Country Boy again. The Good Lord willing, I will be ninety years old in July 2006. He has answered my prayers over and over again that I would be able to remain healthy, mentally and physically, to provide for my wife and family. I truly thank My Almighty God for all of the many, many blessings He has bestowed on me.

Don, Pete, Ronna, Jack, Pat, & Lynn

AND NOW "THE REST OF HIS STORY": HIS CHILDREN REMEMBER

Daddy told several stories of his childhood over the years that we always enjoyed hearing. Granny Newton raised all eleven children by herself. One day Uncle Roy did something and was sure he would be punished, so he ran from her. She said, "Run, Son, run; chickens always come home to roost." Later that night, when all the kids were asleep, she went to Uncle Roy's room and opened the window just slightly, so he would be able to get back into the house. Then she went to bed. Uncle Roy came home, slipped in through the window, and crawled into bed, sure his mother was asleep. Once he was asleep, Granny got up and went to his bed. There were no fitted sheets back then! She quietly undid each corner of the bed sheets, pulled the opposing corners and tied them together around Uncle Roy; and then began to whip him. He awoke but had no way out, and she whipped him good, saying: "I told you chickens come home to roost!" –*Ronna*

Another one about Uncle Roy: Once as a young boy, Uncle Roy was sitting in the door of the corn crib in one of the barns. As he sat, he was leisurely tossing some corn to the chickens in the barnyard. Granddaddy passed by, noticed what was happening, and said to Uncle Roy, "Don't do that, Son." Uncle Roy misunderstood him to say, "Throw it to 'em, Son." So, he began really "throwin' it to 'em!" Granddaddy, of course, did not tolerate disobedience, and without any hesitation, he wore the seat of Uncle Roy's britches out. This must have made as big an impression on Daddy as it did on Uncle Roy because Daddy always tried to be sure he understood the situation before punishment was rendered upon us. *–Lynn*

Another of Dad's stories: One day his sister Ada and brother Roy were out with the cows and their calves. They decided to tie the calves' tails together and then couldn't get them undone. Ada came to the house and got a butcher knife to cut them apart. As she turned around to go back to the barn, Granny said: "What you gonna do with that knife?" Ada immediately replied, "Cut hot butter!" *–Ronna*

Another story Daddy told: One day when they were quite young, Uncle Raleigh and Uncle Harvey were playing out in the yard using the ax to chop corn cobs in half to make them pop up. Uncle Harvey had the ax. Uncle Raleigh stuck his foot out and dared Uncle Harvey to chop his toe off! Uncle Raleigh didn't believe for a minute that Uncle Harvey would do it–and Uncle Harvey didn't believe that Uncle Raleigh would leave his foot there! Well, Uncle Raleigh did, and Uncle Harvey did! He chopped his toe–not off–but right down the middle! *–Lynn*

Another of his memories: One day Dad's sister Ada had done something for which Granny felt she needed to be punished. As Granny whipped her, Aunt Ada said, "Is that the best you can do, ole woman?" To which Granny begin to pray aloud; "If I must fight; if I should reign, increase my courage, Lord!" never missing a beat with the whip. Granny's prayer was answered, and Aunt Ada began to beg, "That's enough, Mama. That's enough! That's enough!"*–Ronna*

After spending a week or two with his grandparents during the summer, my son Brad came home and said, "Mama, you know Granddaddy doesn't see too well out of those eyes in the front of his head, but he has perfect vision in those eyes in the back of his head." –*Pat*

Daddy's eyes could be like daggers, too! Especially in church. Mama sang in the choir, and Daddy always sat on the third pew from the front on the right side of the aisle with five children; and there was never any doubt he had control. If we misbehaved, our conscience would make us look to see if Daddy was watching. He never had to call us down–he looked us down! He didn't have to say a word. With one of those looks, we were in big trouble! –*Lynn*

Daddy was a strict disciplinarian. He didn't beat us, but he did punish us to accomplish training and respect. Once, after having spent over two hours increasing our pent-up energy in church, Pete and I got somewhat rowdy when we got home and entered the house. Mom stopped in the kitchen to finish dinner. Daddy picked up a flyswatter to kill flies in the kitchen. This particular old flyswatter had a heavy gauge wire handle with a thin piece of cloth fabric sewn around the metal wire mesh screen swatting surface–except the stitching had unraveled at one corner of the swatting surface, exposing the jagged edge of the metal screen on that corner. As Pete and I entered our bedroom to change from Sunday pants to play clothes, petty bickering escalated to low-grade yelling and pushing and shoving. My scream of pain brought Daddy into the room, armed with the flyswatter. I quickly complained that Pete was picking on me, and Pete complained in return. I was fully expecting Daddy to "word-whip" both of us for being too rowdy, but without a word and without warning, Daddy slashed the jagged-edged fly-swatter across the back of both our bare legs and quietly said, "Stop your nonsense and come to dinner!" He immediately left the room with both Pete and me standing speechless. *–Don*

I learned about "the birds and the bees" from Daddy. The day before I started the 8th grade, he, and he alone, drove me to Charlotte, North Carolina, to get glasses. Daddy always had "method in his madness", and I'm sure this was one of those times! It's 100 miles from our house to Charlotte, so it took a good two hours. Coming back, it seemed like four! Daddy picked this time to tell me all about things I really didn't want to hear. He talked all the way home. I don't believe I said a word the entire way home. When we got home, to the barnyard we went. He told me about all the animals, and then proceeded to draw pictures in the dirt. At the end of his "lesson" (he is speaking of pregnancy), he tries to break the tension by saying to me, "And if you put your ear close, you can hear '*Thump. Thump. Thump*'. What do you think that is?" I very timidly respond, as he knew I would, "I guess it's the baby's heart beating." To which he comes back with, "No! The baby has the hic-ups!" I was so embarrassed! *–Lynn*

I was the most disobedient, defiant of the five children, I think. Momma really hated to punish us but would on occasion. She had on more than one occasion slapped me in the mouth for sassing her. One particular night, she wanted me to say, "Yes Ma'am." I refused. She got more and more upset demanding that I say, "Yes Ma'am." I got more and more defiant–that is, until Daddy walked in the door and saw and heard what was going on. Momma was in tears, and in short order so was I. Daddy did not tolerate disrespect of Momma, much less defiance and back talk in a child. He took the fly swatter and he tore my little butt up! –*Ronna*

Daddy was always taking opportunities to teach. One day when I was rather young and riding in the truck with him, we approached the railroad tracks near our house. Dad asked me what was coming, and I responded: "N-u-h....t-h-i-n'. . . (long pause) . . .but a train." By this time, we were on the tracks and the train getting close. Not a good time for southern drawl! –*Pete*

Pete got married on April 17th. Standing on the front porch of Boykin Methodist Church, just before going down the aisle, Daddy said to me: "This is a ridiculous time of year for you to be getting married. Every farmer who is here should be out plowing his fields today."–*Pat*

As a young lad, I dearly loved television cowboy shows. One stunt they did was, upon hearing an urgent issue, they'd dash out of the saloon, unhitch and point their horse out of town while grabbing the saddle horn with both hands; and as the horse galloped out of town, the cowboy would plant both his feet firmly on the ground. The speed of the horse and the firm implantation of the feet would catapult the cowboy into the saddle, and he'd ride out of town. That was the coolest thing to this ten-year-old, and I wanted to emulate that feat. Daddy had a five-gated saddle horse named Black Beauty, and Beauty always returned to the barn wide open. Daddy would always say that while we were riding, if anything happened, just hold onto the saddle horn and Beauty would bring us home. Knowing that she would bolt to the barn when the reigns were loosed, I'd lead her to the house, turn her toward the barn, and put one foot into the stirrup. And since I was too short to hold, plant and spin into the saddle, I'd grab the horn, and loose the reins. She'd bolt toward the barn as I held the horn. I'd plant the trailing foot, swing up into the saddle, and pull her to the side of the barn and on down the lane. I know. . .I know. . .it wasn't as fancy as the TV stuntmen, but in my mind, I was doing it!

One day, Daddy was straightening a nail on the anvil that was positioned between the house and the barn. Without telling him what I was going to do, I positioned Beauty for the launch. As the reigns loosened and we lifted off, the movement must have caught Daddy's eye. Apparently, all he saw was a runaway horse with me hanging off the side. As Beauty was about to run by him, I was completely airborne–swinging up into the saddle. Daddy stepped into the horse's path, hit her right between the eyes while he simultaneously grabbed both reigns directly beneath the bridle bit and jerked them backwards, yelling, "Where do you think you're going!" As he struck her, she planted all four feet in front of her and stopped on a dime, followed immediately by going into full reverse with the jerk of the bit, and she was groaning through it all. Remember, I was airborne with a forward vector when she stopped and reversed. Thus, my body went over the saddle horn and my hands that clasped it, planting my face between her ears, laying my torso along her neck with my legs straddling my arms and the base of her neck. Daddy jerked her backwards again, admonishing her not to try it again. As he did so, her body motion catapulted me up and back over the horn into the saddle. Daddy asked if I was alright, and as I tried to assimilate what went wrong, I said, "Yes sir!" He replied, "I don't think she'll ever try that again." And I said, "No sir. I promise you she won't!" I never told Daddy that I had put her up to it. I walked her out of Daddy's sight, got off, and face to face, made the most heart-felt apology a guy has ever given his trusty steed. Daddy was right–I never asked her to do that stunt again. –*Don*

We all learned to drive under Daddy's leadership. We girls usually began by sitting in Daddy's lap to "drive" home from church. As we grew and could reach the floorboard, we began to use the gas and the brake. All we had was stick-shift vehicles, so we had to learn how to change gears using the clutch. All the jerking and the times we choked down kept us in hysterics. At the base of a huge Sweet Gum tree in our yard, was, and still is today, an old "hitching post". It was used to hitch your horse before there were cars. One day, when Pat was learning to drive, as she began to turn the steering wheel (this is before power steering) into the circle driveway, she couldn't get it turned good enough. She thought she was going to hit the tree and the hitching post, so she just turned loose of the steering wheel, threw both arms up in the air, and yelled, "Bam!" No brakes–nothing–just "Bam!" Daddy grabbed the wheel and hit the brake, and all was O.K. Over time we mastered the process, driving the truck and tractor, as well as the car. Dad always stressed safety and the things we were not to do.

One day he decided that we should all learn how to change a tire on an automobile if we were going to drive. He took the car to the front driveway and showed us the entire process in detail. We each had to take turns until he was satisfied, we could change a tire. It wasn't the easiest thing for me (Ronna), because I didn't weigh much, so I had to jump up and down on the lug wrench to loosen (and tighten) the lugs. At some point he also taught us how to check the oil and add more if necessary. I don't believe any of us have ever forgotten, and while we seldom have to change a tire, we could today if we needed to. Dad's love was demonstrated in caring that his children were prepared when out in the world and alone. *–Ronna and Lynn*

When Daddy went to take the tobacco to the "tobacco market", (where they auction a huge warehouse full of cured and graded tobacco) he would usually take some or all of us with him. He would sit each one of us on a separate basket of his tobacco, which made us really feel special. He would tell us girls to "Look real pretty, now," and that our sitting there real pretty would make his tobacco bring more money per pound. Don remembers him telling the boys to say to the buyers as the auction "line" approached, "Help me out, boys. This is for my college." Or "Help me out, boys. I need new shoes for school." Daddy would always use any psychological ploy to sneak an extra dime out of those buyers! Listening to the auctioneers was quite an experience, not to mention that they would always make some complimentary comment about us as they prepared to auction Daddy's "special" baskets. *–Lynn, Ronna, and Don*

One of Mama's cousins produces some of the best sweet potatoes in the state. One day, Daddy put a tobacco basket (about 4 to 4½ feet sq.) in the trunk of the car, went to visit the cousin, and overloaded that basket with sweet potatoes. On his way home, he saw this huge rattlesnake coiled in the road. The only weapon he had was a foot long L-shaped lug wrench. He threw that wrench at the snake and pinned its head to the pavement! The snake was about six feet long, and probably six-eight inches in circumference. Daddy coiled that big presumably dead snake on top of the sweet potatoes and proceeded home.

He stopped in Bennettsville to show some guys his snake. When he opened the trunk, his potatoes were all over the place, and the snake had moved! His snake was not really dead! There's an old saying that snakes don't die until the sun goes down, so Daddy went on home and left his snake to die. The next morning Daddy told Don to get the .22 rifle and go kill the snake, but Don found the snake was already dead. Later that morning, Daddy took his "prize" snake to the county newspaper where they made his picture holding that snake and put the article in the paper! –Lynn and Don

If you've gotten nothing else from this book, you should know Daddy is a very proud man; and he has every right to be. He has always done everything he attempted to the best of his ability. His military career has always been special, and what he learned from all of the experiences told in this book, and those left untold, were used in teaching us children something about life. His experience was the main reason I ended up at Clemson in Air Force R.O.T.C. I remember the pride he exuberated upon my graduation and commissioning. He and my future wife, Libby, each pinned a bar on my shoulders. I am not sure who was proudest that day, but I'm also not sure it was me. –Pete

As a ranking officer in the Army, Daddy got things done by pushing his "rank" around and continued doing it in civilian life. He taught us to assume the authority in a situation, even if we didn't have it. Most people will allow you to "get it done". But he always did it in such a way that those around him didn't notice, or at least, didn't get offended. Back then, we went for dental work as a family with no "reservations", but he just went up to the office clerk, told them we had traveled a distance to get there, and we needed to be seen right then so we could get back home. Suddenly, one of us would be called for our checkup, then the other, and soon, we'd be on our way! Or when matriculating in college, we might have been told that we couldn't do one thing before the other, even though we had waited in that line for a time before getting to the point where someone could tell us that. Daddy would "reason" with their supervisor, who would lead us around the background and get us totally matriculated without any lines. We never went to any gathering that Daddy didn't demonstrate this characteristic in some fashion. I have observed that each of his children possesses and has demonstrated this trait in some form in our adult life. –Don

When I (Lynn) was about fourteen or fifteen years old, Daddy got hit on the head with the sickle mower blade that he and Milton York (one of the farm workers) were attaching to the tractor. The blade was approximately eight feet long, stood upright while traveling, and was slowly lowered to lie just below the grass to mow. The blade was in the upright position, when the connecting rod holding it up broke. The blade fell quickly, hitting Daddy right in the top of his head, bursting his skull, and knocking him out. This scared Milton, and everyone else, to death! I'm sure he thought Daddy was dead. He looked at Daddy and froze. Our cousin R.L. ran to the house to tell Mama. Mama ran out and told Milton to go get the car (the keys were always left in it), and ran back in to get towels, etc., for Daddy until they could get him to the hospital. Milton had Daddy in the car and was driving ("flying low") out through the yard headed to the hospital. Mama had to flag him down to stop for her. Mama said he drove like a maniac all the way to the hospital in Bennettsville–ten miles away. Sister Pat was very young and was screaming uncontrollably. We, the other children, could not seem to quiet her. We were all scared and crying, afraid our daddy would die. They were gone the better part of the day. When they returned, Daddy was with them, but his head was wrapped up with white bandages, and he was weak and pale. He was told to take it easy and not to drive for a while.

One Saturday morning after that, he needed part from a farm equipment store about ten miles away. There was no-one available to drive him, so he told me (Lynn) I had to take him. I had my driver's permit and maybe even my license, but I was still really not confident enough to do much driving. But he insisted we had to go—and we had to go right now! The place was to close in about fifteen minutes. I very hesitantly and cautiously began driving. He told me we had to hurry. The store would close before we got there, so "step on it". I just couldn't make myself go as fast as he wanted me to, and he just kept pressuring me. For the first time in my life, I came "this close" to telling him off! Of course, I didn't, but I felt like it! We made it in time, but we were both really stressed by the time we got there. —*Lynn and Ronna*

My Daddy grew up as part of The Greatest Generation. But it didn't come without a cost. Daddy fought in Europe during World War II and was emotionally wounded with tragic memories of losing close buddies, of bodies being ripped apart, of blood-curdling screams of pain, of groans of the dying on the battlefield, and forever wondering why it was them and not him. He was also wounded physically when a German soldier fired an anti-aircraft gun at close range, and the bullet almost destroyed his right hand. It was saved by a doctor who heard Daddy's plea not to take it. That old veteran tried a unique, experimental procedure where he attached all vessels on one side of the wound to a single vein. That single vein feeds the extremities of his right hand and keeps it alive to-day. It saved Daddy's hand but left it very tender. Every time he meets someone, he extends his left hand, not his right, for the traditional handshake to protect his right hand. I never knew just how sensitive it was until one day while trying to "break" a nut on the engine of the car, his wrench slipped, and he hit his hand against the head of an engine bolt. Daddy shrieked in pain, jerked his hand out, grasped it with his left hand and held it tightly between his legs as he fell to the ground in the fetal position where he writhed in pain for about ten minutes and convulsively cried. I was about fourteen years old, and I knelt down beside him and tried to comfort him as I cried with him. For the first time, I appreciated some of the pain he had suffered for my generation's freedom and had carried with him for his entire adult life. *–Don*

For Daddy's seventy-fifth birthday, we decided to surprise him and meet for lunch. We chose a restaurant, and all of us with our children were to meet there for the surprise. It was up to Don and his wife Pat to see that Daddy and Mama were there. We all arrived on that Sunday at the restaurant, only to find out that we could not have a private dining room, nor could we hold enough seats in the main dining room for the clan. There was another restaurant across the street, and we decided to check that out. They offered us a private room with lots of space, so our location plans quickly changed. Now we had a major problem. Don and Pat did not know of the change, and they were bringing Daddy and Mama.

One of the grandchildren, who was a private detective at that time, was known to show up just about anywhere on a case he was working. He decided to stay at the original restaurant, act surprised when he "just happened" to run into

Daddy and Mama, and convince them to go across the street for lunch together. When Don pulled into the parking lot, the grandchild spotted them, nonchalantly "ran into them", told them that this restaurant was too crowded, and they should go across the street.

Well, Daddy would have nothing to do with that idea. He said he had eaten at the other place one time in his life, and that had been his first time and his last! With much coaxing, he was finally talked into trying it out once more. After all, it had been several years since he first had eaten there.

We were all in the private dining room waiting when the hostess directed Daddy and Mama there to be seated. They both were quite surprised to see all of us, and we all had a wonderful time (and good food) to help Daddy celebrate his special day. –Pat

Jack, Ethell & children – Jack's 75th Birthday

I always thought of Mama as being the one who most instilled in us our Christian values, but there was one instance I remember where Daddy really got my attention. Our cousin Ria Lee Blake was visiting, and she and I wanted the car to go to Bennettsville one night. When I asked Daddy if we could go, he replied: "The Bible says, 'Ask and it shall be given you.' If you can find the rest of that verse of scripture in the Bible, you may have use of the car." It took us about an hour, but we did find the verse, Matthew 7:7, and were allowed to go out that night. *–Pat*

Daddy constructed a two-story cinder-block building behind the house. The ground level floor was three separate rooms, two of which were used for storage of home-canned goods, and for hanging country hams to cure, etc. The third room was on the end of the building. It contained two iron "wash pots" built into a concrete oven (fire pit). The pots were used to heat water for washing clothes and "killing hogs". Above these three rooms is one long room with windows on each side and a door on each end. It was to be used as a "pack house" to grade tobacco. Daddy had a beautiful hardwood floor installed and shellacked, and when completed, it gleamed like gold! He thought it looked like a great place to have a dance. So that's what we did. We lived way out in the country and few friends other than cousins had ever been to our home, so we were ecstatic! We invited cousins, friends, schoolmates, and Sunday School friends. . .and we had us a "Barn Dance", and a great time that Saturday night. After that, it became the "pack house". We children were taught to grade tobacco and did that every summer for many years. Of course, in everything there was a lesson. "If it's worth doing, it's worth doing right." We learned that work didn't kill you—that it could actually be enjoyed (fun). We learned that perseverance paid off, and that we should take pride in a job well done. —*Lynn and Ronna*

One of my favorite Christmases was the year Ronna, Pete, and I all three got bicycles. We children also got a fantastic official-type basketball goal, which was made by the agriculture class of the high school. It seemed huge! But it was perfect in every way and made to exact specifications of legality. Granny Newton lived with us; and Aunt Vida was visiting, as well as were Aunt Lucille and Uncle Bob and their three children.

Mama and Daddy "had their reason" and decided this Christmas Eve would be special. Mama, Aunt Lucille, and all eight of the children were going to go caroling. Daddy and Uncle Bob "weren't home", so they didn't "get to go". Well, caroling we went! Uncle Raleigh and his family lived about a mile away; and Uncle Roy and his family lived about a mile and a half away in a different direction. And, of course, there were neighboring friends and tenant farmers all around. Being out in the country, it wasn't like any of us were "next door", however. We stopped at every house we came to—and sang all the songs we could think of at each house. We never got out of the car, but we sang to houses where the lights were on. We sang to houses where people were asleep. We even sang to houses where nobody lived! We sang forever! Just before we got back home, we saw an airplane fly over. Mama wondered if that was Santa Claus in an airplane instead of a sleigh! *"Wonder if Santa Claus came while we were out?"* *"Wonder what that would be like?"* Well, when we got home, we found out! Santa Claus had indeed come while we were out caroling! Boy! Eight children coming home to "Santa Claus". We were beyond excitement! Aunt Vida and Granny came out in their nightclothes wondering what in the world was going on. Daddy and Uncle Bob came in the house questioning all the commotion, exclaiming they could hear us all the way out to the barnyard. What an experience! But there were a couple of pitfalls to our excitement: None of the children wanted to go to bed! And then, we wouldn't and couldn't go to sleep! That did it for caroling on Christmas Eve! *–Lynn*

In early spring, after we all received the bikes for Christmas, the school bus had to turn around in our drive when it let us off at home. The county had dumped large loads of dirt in three or four places along the road between our home and the Bennettsville highway–about a mile–in preparation to pave the road. We begged Daddy to let us give the Odom children a ride on home on the bikes. He said, "You may take them home but stay off the mounds of dirt. Do not get on them, understand?" We said, "Yes, Sir," and took them home. On the way back, we rode back and forth across those dirt mounds. It was so much fun, until we rode into the yard. Daddy was standing under the big gum tree holding a switch. He had been watching us do exactly what he told us not to do. He made that switch speak as nothing else across the calves of my legs, and that wasn't the last time either! Daddy had a policy: speak to you once and if he had to speak twice, the second time was "two feet off the ground". Daddy didn't tolerate disobedience. *–Ronna*

As Christmas approached, about mid-December, Daddy would get his gloves and the old ax and take us kids to the woods to find the "best" Christmas tree. He showed us how to check all sides of the tree, to get the most perfect to decorate. Once found, he would cut it near the base, drag it to the truck, load it and bring it home. He would sink it in an old clay-fired pot filled with wet sand (for many years we didn't have a tree stand; that would come years later) and leave it to Mom and the kids to decorate. Most times it was cedar, but sometimes it was pine. Always it was special and beautiful.

We children were not bought some toy every time we went to a store, nor did we beg and throw tantrums for things. However, Christmas was always "huge" at the Newton home, at least in the eyes of this child. On Christmas Eve each of us would select a pan (we didn't hang a stocking), put our name in the bottom, and place it in a chair in the living room where the Christmas tree stood. That way, Santa knew what toys, etc. to leave where and filled our pans with fruit, nuts, and candy. There was a heavy door with a large keyhole that opened to the hall off from the bedrooms. Very early on Christmas morning, we would awaken and run to the hall door of the living room, and peak through the keyhole to see if Santa had been. Of course, he always had; but there was Dad on his knees, with the hint of a drip on his nose, at the old stove heater in his drab green army fatigues, army boots, gloves, and cap that had the flap pulled down over his ears. He had the coal bucket and "fat-lighter" kindling starting a fire so we could enjoy Christmas morning in warmth and comfort! We saw sacrificial love in action! *–Ronna and Pat*

As much as humanly possible, my Daddy treated all people with respect and dignity. I saw this trait all my life, but never more than the summer of 1976 when I visited with Momma and Daddy for several weeks while recovering from hepatitis. One July Sunday afternoon, a car turned into our drive. Daddy went out to greet whoever had arrived. He approached the car with a wide grin on his face and began to entreat the occupants to come in and make themselves at home. As the driver exposed his identity, Daddy recognized him as one of his all-time favorite relatives on Momma's side of the family. Daddy's demeanor and the exuberance of his voice never changed from his first expressions before he even knew who he was greeting. As they departed after a two-hour visit, Daddy walked them to their car and told them how honored we were to have had them visit. Less than fifteen minutes later, another car arrived, and Daddy began greeting them exactly the same. However, he soon recognized the couple as one of those for whom he had much less regard among his own relatives, but again, Daddy's demeanor and the exuberance of his voice never changed from his first expressions before he even knew who he was greeting. He invited them to come in and make themselves at home. They remained in the car, saying they could only stay a few moments. Daddy squatted down so that he'd be at eye level with the couple. He stayed in that position, shifting his weight from side to side to avoid muscle fatigue, and visited with that couple for almost one and a half hours. And as they began to leave, Daddy told them how honored we were to have had them visit. Two couples who dropped by for a visit and left feeling they were THE most important people in my father's life. I saw him welcome visitor after visitor—family, friends, sharecroppers, and strangers—all the same throughout my whole life and still to this very day. He respected all persons. –*Don*

Growing up on a farm led to many experiences that others were not as fortunate to have had as we. I remember quite often standing around watching Daddy milk the cow, her tail swishing in Daddy's face; and her feet stomping—sometimes kicking over the milk bucket. Many times, Daddy would squeeze the milk straight from the cow's teat into our mouths. It was really fun, but I believe that's when I decided I'd rather have my milk cold! *–Lynn*

Daddy was always taking moments that he hardly had time to spare to teach us something. Most would be important to us in our future lives, though we could not imagine it at the time. It may have been about honesty, which he demanded of us; dependability, which he had to have from all of us to know things would be done on the farm; respect, of not just him and Mom, but all of our elders as well as everyone else; politeness or consideration, or any of the other things mentioned above and by my brother and sisters. He made sure we got an education–formal book sense from school, and good common sense from home. *–Pete*

Each fall our Methodist Youth Fellowship would have a hayride. It was always in October and usually the night of the full moon. I don't remember anyone but Daddy ever being in charge. He would load the big open wagon with lots of hay from the farm and hook it up to the mules or the tractor and drive us around a couple of hours for a fun ride. Late October could be quite cold, so that, along with the full moon, would give some of us a good excuse to "snuggle" if there happened to be a little infatuation amongst us! For one of those hayrides, "Nellie", the work horse was used to pull the wagon. She was really close to giving birth to a foal (her son, "Blaze"). She was so close that she actually began to give birth before Daddy could get her back to the barn. Close call! *–Lynn*

Every summer, we would swap weeks going to visit cousins. One or more of us would go visit with them for a week, bringing back one or more of them to spend a week with us. We swapped off until most of us from both sides of the family (Daddy's and Mama's) had all visited each summer. One summer, Mama and Daddy had all of the cousins (probably close to two dozen) at our house the same week. That only happened once, however! Daddy always treated them as if they were his own children, demanding and getting the same respect from each of them as he did from us. If he didn't, they got a whippin', just as we did or would have. He fully believed in "Spare the rod and spoil the child." And he took the time to "teach" our cousins, as he had us, how to perform the farm chores that kept us all busy and out of trouble.

When we went to Andrews, South Carolina, (Mama's hometown) often we would ride the train. Andrews was a big train town, as was Hamlet, North Carolina. Hamlet is about 10 miles from our house, so our parents would take us to the train stations to go visit back and forth with only the supervision of the train conductors. One time, Pete and I rode alone to Andrews. I'm thinking I was about eight years old and Pete about five—we may have been even younger. Pete had fallen asleep with his head in my lap during the trip. The conductor came through selling Coca-Colas. He was calling out, "Coca-Cola! Coca-Cola! Anybody want Coca-Cola?" As he got close to me, I raised my hand, and he asked me if I wanted a Coke. I shook my head, "Yes," and he put his container down, took out one bottle Coke (eight-ounces, which is how they were sold at that time), took his bottle opener and popped the cap right off. He handed it to me—Pete still asleep in my lap—and said, "That'll be ten cents, please." I was shocked! I had no idea it was going to cost me! I told him, "I ain't got no money." Then he was shocked! But he left the Coca-Cola with me and went on down the aisle smiling. —*Lynn*

Dr. Tommy Gibson was not only our local doctor, but also a good friend to Daddy and Mama. Mama had become quite the avid fisherman, and Dr. Gibson had a pond where he allowed very few to fish. He gave Mama and Daddy permission to use the pond anytime they desired. One July 3rd, Daddy had gone to fish Doc's pond without telling Mama. While fishing, he found one spot in the pond that seemed to be the "honey spot" for brim, which was one of Mama's favorite fish.

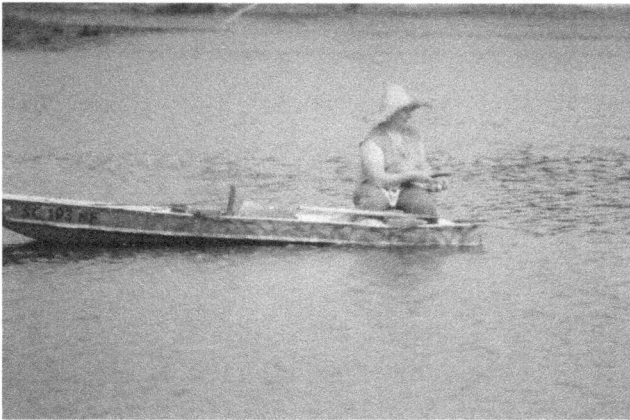

Ethell fishing on Doc's pond

The next day, July 4th, Daddy suggested they go fishing, and Mama quickly "took the bait". They used just a regular paddle boat—Mama in the front and Daddy in the back. Daddy paddled to the secret "honey spot", but to his frustration, Mama kept fishing the opposite side of the boat. Daddy "suggested" several times that she try the other side, but when she didn't, his frustration grew until he snapped to her, "Ethell, will you just cast over there! Will you just cast OVER THERE! CAST OVER THERE, ETHELL!" She re-baited her hook with one of those healthy, nice, live crickets they were using, and threw it backward in order to "chunk it" into the water, as Daddy had told her to do so many times before. She suddenly felt a really heavy pull against her "chunk". She had hooked Daddy right in the cartilage between the nostrils of his nose. The line never got "chunked", and up Daddy's nose the cricket wiggled! When Mama realized she had "hooked" Daddy, all she could do was pitifully say, "Oh! Jack. Oh! Jack. Oh! Jack." And if anybody ever heard Mama say, "Oh! Jack," you can still hear her, in her special way, saying it today. Daddy didn't know whether to laugh or cry!

They made it back to the bank with Daddy still sharing his nose with the cricket and the fishhook. Remember, this is the 4th of July. It took them quite a long time, but they finally managed to find Dr. Gibson at his home, where Doc met them at the door with a flashlight in his hand. As Doc opened the door, Daddy said, "Doc, I smell a cricket!" Dr. Gibson shined the flashlight up Daddy's nose and replied, "Damn, if I don't believe you do!"

They went to his office where Dr. Gibson turned to Mama and asked, "You really want me to do this? You've finally got Jack right where you want him. All you have to do is tug on this fishing line (as he demonstrates), and he'll go where you want him to go, and do what you want him to do!" Without giving Mama a chance to respond, Daddy says to Dr. Gibson, "For Pete's sake, Doc, would you get this cricket out of my nose?" Daddy enjoyed telling this story as much as any he ever told. It was so funny, and Mama would laugh so hard it would bring tears to her eyes. He'd always tell us (and others), "Your Mama hooked me twice in fifty years. . .once when we got married, and once with a fishhook!" *—Pat, Lynn, Don, Ronna, and Pete*

Daddy was apparently all-knowing as he always seemed to find out the things we did but shouldn't have done. I began driving the tractor around the farm when I was six or seven years old and on the highways to the repair shops before I was ten. I got my driver's license when I was fifteen, but they "restricted" my driving to between 6:00 a.m. and 6:00 p.m. Because of a situation in the school system, I ended up classified a junior in high school when I was only fifteen years old while all other juniors were sixteen and possessed unrestricted licenses. The class planned a party to be held about five miles from our home. Knowing that I'd only have to travel country roads to get there and that all my friends would drive themselves, I asked Daddy to allow me to drive. He didn't want to but yielded on one condition. I must go directly to and from the party. I MUST NOT go into town. I agreed, and no sooner entered the party than my best friends began to pressure me to drive into town to get a burger after the party. All night they bugged me, and I told them I could not. To placate them, I suggested that I'd follow them to the burger joint, but then I'd have to go straight home. They agreed. When I circled the burger joint, I must have run over broken glass or something, because as I pulled back out on the highway, my left rear tire was flat.

Well, whoever had used the Valiant jack last, had stored it tightly, and I couldn't loosen it. While I was bent over into the trunk working on it, a Highway Patrolman pulled right up behind me. Not wanting to tell him I wasn't licensed to drive at eleven o'clock at night, I told him I could handle it. Well, he helped get the jack loose, and with his big four-way lug wrench, proceeded to "spin" all the lugs off while I jacked the car up. After the tire was changed, he surveyed all the other tires, each of which was slick as glass. (Daddy would run 'em until you could see the air in 'em!) He asked if Daddy knew the tires were slick. I told him that we lived on a farm, and that Daddy allowed the tires to wear and then move them onto the farm trailers. And furthermore, Daddy had just remarked that it was about time to move these tires to the flatbed trailer. He told me to tell Daddy that he personally said for Daddy to change those tires. When I got home, Momma and Daddy were already asleep.

At breakfast the next morning Daddy, having already been out on the farm, asked, "Did everything go alright last night?" I said, "Yes, sir." A few minutes passed, and he asked, "Did you have any trouble?" I said, "No, sir." A few more minutes passed, and he quietly said, "I thought I taught you how to change a tire." And I asked, "How did you know about that?" He said, "That's not important. You just remember that you can never go anywhere or do anything that I won't find out about!"

When I graduated from college, Daddy asked me to summarize how he did as a parent raising me. I said, "Daddy, I just want to know one thing–who told you about the patrolman changing that tire for me five years ago?" He said, "I'll never tell you." I pressed him a little, and he said, "To tell you the truth, I've forgotten." I asked him again years later, and he didn't remember the situation, much less who told him. That thing still bugs me to this day! –*Don*

Daddy, beginning early in our young lives, would tell us that if we wouldn't smoke a cigarette or drink a drop of whiskey or alcohol by the time, we turned eighteen years old or graduated from high school, whichever came first, he would give us $100! He would repeat this often to remind us not to drink or smoke. He would also pull out a $1 bill and some matches, strike the match and hold it just below the $1 bill and ask us if we wanted him to burn the money. He told us that was what we did when we lit a cigarette. We were burning money, just throwing it away. He would also say that if we would study smart, work hard and help him not waste or spend money needlessly, that one day we would have inheritance and something to show for all the work and sacrifice. I graduated from high school before I turned eighteen, and when Daddy asked me to look him in the eye and tell him that I had never smoked or drank whiskey, I couldn't do it. I looked him in the eye and told him that I couldn't lie to him, that I had tried cigarettes (on my senior trip to N.Y. and Washington), but not whiskey. He gave me the $100 for not telling a lie. And true to his word as always, he has provided through all these years our every need and many of our wants. Yes, and an inheritance of money, but a better inheritance than that–the wonderful love of a Dad for his children. We are all closely bonded as family, educated, successful, productive members of society, with children and grandchildren of our own. *–Ronna*

There were so many things that Daddy said and did that were so very wise. Of course, there were also quite a few things that seemed somewhat stupid, but he probably doesn't want those published. During the summer of my junior year in high school, one of my cousins visited, and Pete, Pat, my cousin, and I begged the car from Daddy and went out for a night on the town. We got into some mischief, one incident of which resulted in smoking cigarettes. Daddy had always bribed us since early childhood, offering $100 if we didn't smoke cigarettes or drink alcohol. We returned home around 10:30 p.m. and settled in the den with Momma and Daddy. Daddy, as usual, was asleep in his recliner, "waiting for the late news to come on."

On the 11 p.m. news, the news broadcaster described a story about drunken youth doing some illegal act. Momma just erupted with comments about how disgusting such activities were, and how God would not bless such youth who chose to live like that, and with her voice escalating in pitch with each sentence, she ended with, "And I hope I never hear of any of my children being involved with cigarettes or alcohol!" At that, she paused, and all of us tried to become invisible by slithering as far down into our seats as possible. But as she sized each of us up, she asked, "Well, have you ever used alcohol or cigarettes?" It was at that precise moment that Daddy, whom we all thought was sound asleep, opened the eye nearest Momma and us (we were all seated to his right) and quietly, with great wisdom, said, "Now, Ethell, if you hope you never hear about them doing it, don't ask 'em if they did, 'cause I ain't gonna let 'em lie to you." Momma was quiet for a moment (going on 5 hours) before finally saying again, "Well, I better not ever hear of it!" And we all breathed a collective sigh of relief! It was one of the many times Daddy's wisdom amazed us. *–Don*

Jack sleeping in his recliner

Dad saw to it that we went to school and that our studies were done. He was on the board of trustees. He gave us quarters for "A's" and was not happy with anything less. He encouraged us to participate in sports. We played basketball and the boys played football. Dad and Mom supported the games and encouraged everything we attempted. Several of us took piano lessons. They were there for the recitals. We were in Glee club, Beta club, FHA & FFA, Key club, Band, 4-H club, etc. When we entered high school, Daddy sent us to school the first day to bring home a schedule of all classes! He would sit us down and personally help us map a schedule that would get every subject offered for that grade and the next three years. Every slot was filled with something. He wanted us to get everything school had to offer and get the best all-around education available.

No study halls or loafing if there was another subject we could take. So, it was throughout all four years of high school. We all graduated with extra credits, something the school officials questioned when tallying all of our curriculum grades for graduation. We also graduated among the top of our class. Daddy knew how hard it was for him growing up, and how important education was to us and our future. He always said he expected the girls would grow up and marry, but it was just as important for them to get an education and be able to make a living if something were to happen to their husbands and leave them on their own with children to raise. –Ronna

We would watch Daddy weigh the cotton that had been picked during the day. Once weighed, it would be loaded two big sheets of cotton in the bed of the pick-up, then four big sheets on top of those two with them balanced out on the truck sides of the bed. Then more sheets stacked on top of those. Dad would ask if we wanted to ride to the gin, and he would let us get way up high on the top of the top sheets and ride while he drove. Once there and while the cotton was being unloaded, he would let us play in the bins of cotton. We were also allowed to ride on the back of the pick-up truck sitting on the tailgate. We would get a big stick and drag it on the dirt roads to make squiggly lines in the dirt or drag a foot if we could stretch that far and still hold on. This would be considered child endangerment today, but what fun we did have and not one of us was ever hurt. *–Ronna*

We girls were always expected to help Mama in the kitchen and with the house cleaning. I remember when, on more than one occasion, we would think that we had managed to get out of washing the supper dishes and went to bed. When Mama would start cleaning up late at night, Daddy would appear in our bedroom, remind us that Mama had worked hard all day, and make us get up, go back to the kitchen, and do the dishes so that Mama could go to bed at a decent hour, too. *–Pat*

One night, in what is now the den, Daddy had us pull up the ladder-back chairs around the old black potbellied stove. He brought in field corn out of the corn crib and had us to rub them together to break the kernels off the cob and into the pail so the chickens could be fed. After the pail was full, Daddy taught us to play a game he called Jack in The Beanstalk. He gave each of us and himself an equal amount of corn kernels, about twenty-thirty pieces. When it was your turn, you picked up secretly from zero, all of your kernels in your cupped hands. With your cupped hands, you tapped your hands on your knee and said, "Jack in the beanstalk, cut him down, how many?" Everyone took a guess. If you had one, and he or she guessed ten, he or she had to give you nine kernels. If you had ten, and ten was guessed, you must give him ten. We played and swapped corn for a long time. It was important time spent with Dad, which was priceless. Another game he liked to play: He would come up behind you, and lovingly slap you in the back (not to hurt) saying "Beat you in the back 'till you have good luck, how many fingers do I hold up?" quickly changing the palm of his hand to zero-five fingers. You then had to guess. He would do this until you guessed correctly the number of fingers he was holding up behind your back. The lesson: Things that had to be done could be made fun.

It doesn't take a lot of money to enjoy life. *—Ronna*

One other example of the hospitality Momma and Daddy exhibited to all was vividly demonstrated when Ray Smith, our long-time County Agent, had a high-ranking government visitor who wanted to audit Ray's work for the day. Ray quickly planned his day so as to "accidentally" arrive at our home around the time he knew that Momma and Daddy ate lunch. As they were approaching the old home place, Ray prepared the official for the sure-to-be-offered invitation for lunch and for the scrumptious meal that would be enjoyed. But Ray had not told Momma and Daddy! That was no problem, because for years he had "happened" by the house at that hour only to have Daddy and Momma share whatever was on the table. When Ray and the official drove up to the back door, they found the screen door shut and the back door wide open. Ray and the official stepped into the house only to find no one at home! But Ray invited the official to have a seat at the table, got the leftovers out of the fridge, heated them up and served them with Daddy's favorite "lemonade tea". The Washington official had never seen anything like it–and was nervously afraid of being arrested for trespassing! Ray told this story for years, the last time being when I visited him a couple weeks before he died. And Momma and Daddy also told the story with much laughter and great pride that they had a friend who would make himself at "home", even in their absence. They were just sorry that they hadn't been there to entertain his official. –*Don*

The spring was planting time, and about May, as we got off the bus after school, we would put our books and things down, change clothes and go barefooted to the field where Dad and the colored help were already at work planting tobacco. Daddy would have a large flatbed truck with tobacco plants and two or three fifty-five-gallon barrels of water parked in the field. He would call to the girls to go to the truck where he would give each of us a large armload of plants and tell us which of the colored ladies, Dinah (affectionately known to all as "Diana"), Eveleigh, etc. we were to drop plants for. The ladies used a "planter", a piece of equipment used to place the tobacco plant in the ground and water it at the same time. Another one of us would then cover the plant as we moved up the row. When we ran out of plants, or the lady would run out of water, we would go to the truck to renew supplies. When one of the children would go to the truck to get more plants, Daddy would say, "Raise your arms and hands up", which we would do. He would then lift us up over the barrels of water, dipping us up and down in the barrel a few times (a special kind of country swimming for children who didn't have pools or lakes or country-club privileges), lift you back out and onto the ground, give you more plants and say, "Now get to work." Daddy always tried to make work fun! He taught us to improvise. It might not be as nice or fancy; but was just as much fun–if not more so! –*Ronna*

One year, Daddy reserved a cottage at Cheraw Beach, the equivalent of a trip to Myrtle Beach today. To a country child it was pure heaven! A whole week of fun in the sun and in the water! Aunt Vera Mae (Momma's sister) and her children went with us, and Momma took "Diana" (who helped her at home all our lives; we thought of Diana much like a second mother) to help out so Momma could enjoy the beach some also. Dad couldn't stay all the time but would come and go when he needed to check on the farm. It was one, if not the only, real vacation week we spent together as a family away from home. We all remember this week with fondness. Usually a ride to the little town of Gibson on Saturday morning and being treated to a coke and a moon pie was our special treat. We weren't given an allowance, but who needed it? *—Ronna*

Ethell, Jack, and Diana

Growing up, Mama and Daddy would occasionally take us to Cheraw State Park for the day to swim. However, those trips were few and far between. On exceptionally hot summer days, Daddy would bring a couple of fifty-five-gallon empty drums up to the back yard for us to fill with water. There was no swimming here, but we could cool off by jumping up and down in the barrel. One year, he dug out watering holes for the cows, and we were allowed to swim in them a few times before he let the cows in. Boy! Was that a gigantic improvement over a fifty-five-gallon drum! Swimming in that watering hole just didn't last long enough, because it was more important to take care of the cows than it was for us to have a little fun! *–Pat*

As sisters Pat and Ronna mentioned in their memories, Daddy let us "swim" in the fifty-five-gallon drums early on, and I was always afraid when I'd go under the water, that as my knees bent inside the drum, they'd become wedged across the diameter of the drum, holding me under until I drowned! Later on, when he had watering holes dug for the cattle, Daddy decided it would be a great place for us to swim. This "hole" was about 18 feet wide and 30 feet long, and it gradually deepened from ground level on the shallow end to about 18 feet deep at the deepest end. However, no one dared try to walk on any part of the bottom because it was covered with a quagmire-type white clay. So, Daddy erected a black creosote post on either side of the hole toward the deeper end and ran a "plow line" (a tightly woven cotton rope about one half inch in diameter that was used to steer a mule while plowing. The rope ran from one side of the mule's bridle bit, around the length of the plow and back to the other side of the bridle bit.) from one pole to the other, allowing the rope to swag down just above the waterline in the center of the hole. He then backed the pick-up right beside one of the poles at the edge of the hole and lowered the tailgate of the truck out to the horizontal position, instructing us to use it as our diving platform. Then, he stood by, serving as lifeguard for us as we dove in, swam, and climbed back out, using the secured rope as our leverage to pull up the steep bank. I couldn't swim and was hesitant about jumping in. But Daddy assured me that he was right there, and that all I had to do was jump in right by the rope and upon surfacing, just reach up and grab the rope. Besides, he was right there if I needed him. I jumped in, grabbed the rope when I surfaced, and never thought twice of it thereafter.

Occasionally, he'd take us to Cheraw State Park to swim in the lake. Since I was also leery of entering that vast expanse of water, he took me into his arms, waded out to where he was on his tiptoes, teaching me to enjoy the water while safe in his arms.

Very seldom did we go to the ocean, and I was really scared of the waves. Once again, Daddy took me into his arms out to where he was on his tiptoes at the lowest ebb of each swell, and he would "bounce" up and let the buoyancy of his body in the surf carry us over each wave; and after it passed, he would balance like a ballerina on his toes until the next wave came.

After I'd graduated from college, we were at a family gathering, and many of us had already been swimming while Daddy sat to watch. After I talked with him for a while, I encouraged him to get in the water with me. When he declined, I pressured him to join us. But he kept declining until finally, he quietly said, "I can't swim.". . .*What did he say?* Did he say. . .I can't. . .I thought I misunderstood, and so I asked him what he said, and he repeated it. He said it very clearly. . .I couldn't believe what I'd heard before, and I said, "Daddy, you can't swim?! What about telling me to dive into the watering hole and you'd be there if 'something happened'? What about Cheraw State Park? Holy smoke, Daddy! What about taking me out over my head and virtually over yours, too, in the ocean where we could both have drowned?

Daddy, what do you mean, you can't swim?" He grinned his little sheepish grin, and said, "You made it, didn't you? Don't worry about it now!" *–Don*

With a large hunting family, Dad was constantly teaching SAFETY! Many times, while hunting he would make me check that my safety was on or correct me for carrying my gun pointing other than up or down. A gun was never to be pointed at anything except what you wanted to kill. Making sure all guns were unloaded before taking them into the house was another point. There were many young non-hunters who didn't know better and might pick up that gun. You were to always make sure your gun was empty (barrel and chamber) before cleaning. I wasn't present for one particular training session, but a very good lesson it was. Dad was going to clean his gun, so he invited all of the "younger" ones (grandchildren) in to teach them while he cleaned. He "KNEW" that gun was empty, but he checked the chamber again for the young ones (but failed to check the barrel). A loaded gun can go off anytime, and you never know who or what is in the line of fire. As Dad sat in the den with the gun pointed towards the window (remember safety), you can imagine his surprise, and that of the little ones, when the gun went off, blowing a hole in the den window, as well as the window in the block house out back. A safety lesson no one ever forgot. *–Pete*

For a long time, Dad shot a sixteen-gauge automatic shotgun with a full choke (pellets held very tight for a long distance), and a thirty-two-inch barrel. With Don and me shooting Improved Cylinder guns (very quick pellet spread), we were quick-draw shooters. A covey of quail would flush and *boom, boom, boom* went Don and me; then *BOOM, BOOM* went Dad. Don and I had to shoot quickly to have a decent chance of hitting a bird. Dad had to wait, or he would blow the bird to pieces. I remember one time at the watering hole where we used to swim by jumping off the back of the pickup, Dad had to stop to blow his always dripping nose. Don and I were taking advantage of the break to rest our guns on the ground (barrels pointed in the air, of course) as they were heavy for us boys. As Dad blew, up comes a covey of quail. Don and I never had a chance to get our guns up, much less on a bird. But Dad, calmly drops his tissue, grabs his gun, takes aim, and drops the bird. –*Pete*

There came a time later in his life when Daddy began deer hunting. To everyone's surprise, he actually killed a deer his very first time! The amazing thing was–they couldn't find any bullet holes. The deer was running away from Daddy, his tail high in the air, and when Daddy shot, the deer ran a couple hundred yards more, and fell. They studied and thought for a long time before determining why that deer showed no signs of bullet entry. You'll probably come to the same conclusion the guys did! –*Lynn*

Daddy loved the outdoors and the sports that took him there. In my early years, he was an avid small game (quail, rabbit, squirrel, and dove) hunter, and always encouraged others to hunt the family farm. He didn't take to fishing much until he was about to retire. In those working years, he was a man on the move, and I think fishing "wasted" his time. I remember begging him to fish with me one time as we vacationed one July 4th week at Uncle Duke's pond. Finally, Daddy consented, and I was already fishing by the time he scrounged a cane pole and came to the pond. He dropped his baited hook in the water, and about five seconds later pulled it out of the pond and lowered it six feet to the left. Five seconds later, he lifted it out of the water and lowered it twelve feet to the right. Five seconds later, he said, "There's nothing here, let's try by the dam." He repeated that scenario about five times as we circled the pond, and he finally grunted, "Humph! Ain't no fish in this pond. Let's go." But when he was close to retiring, and certainly, afterwards, he really enjoyed bass fishing and got to be pretty good at it. He, also, took up deer hunting with his good friends John Barrington and Dr. Tommy Gibson. But as much as he loved the outdoors (he said it taught him a lot about people; and learning how the rabbits hid and evaded the foxes and dogs helped him survive while evading and fighting in World War II), and as much as he loved hunting and fishing, the most memorable part of Daddy's outdoors experiences was listening to him tell the tales of the hunt, the kill, and the catch. No one could spin a tale with as much enthusiasm as my Daddy. –*Don*

We swept the yards, which had no grass, with "broom straw" brooms. This particular chore was done on Saturday, so our yard was pretty on Sunday. We would sweep the leaves and twigs up and then play in them before we piled them back up for Daddy to burn. During the week however, we had twigs and leaves falling again. There were seven or eight pecan trees in the yard, and in late fall it turned cold, but that's when the pecans were falling to the ground. Daddy would have Momma bundle us up good and send us outside. He would give us buckets, and we were to pick up the pecans out of all that yard trash. Sometimes Momma would rake them in small piles so we could use the milk stool or some other small item to sit on while we gathered the pecans. Of course, Dad felt he should help the process along, so he would get a ladder and climb up into the tree, go out a way on a limb, brace himself good, and stomp on the limb as hard as he could so the pecans would fall. Or he would pull a limb down with his hands and shake it to make them fall. It was like a hailstorm on us! It seemed it took all day to get up the nuts. Momma then wanted them shelled for pies, cakes, and goodies. Daddy was still climbing those pecan trees well into his seventies! *–Ronna and Lynn*

Speaking of climbing, I remember when hurricane Hazel came through. Momma gathered all the children and took us to her bed where she sheltered us while the storm passed. But Daddy, all 130 pounds of him, was standing near the top of a ladder that he had laid against the roof, leaning across it onto the roof thinking he could keep the roof and shingles from blowing off during the hurricane. *–Ronna*

For all of my life, Daddy wore army khakis for his farm work clothes. He said they held up better than any other clothes he could buy. The khakis were not the problem. It was that old army green winter jacket that I hated. When I was in high school, he called home from Bennettsville one day, saying he had a flat tire and he needed me to bring him a tire jack from home. When I arrived at where he was stranded, he wouldn't let me leave until he had the tire changed. I remember standing there with him in that old green jacket, hoping that none of my friends would come by because I was embarrassed at the clothes Daddy was wearing. I told him of my embarrassment. He apologized to me and from then on, if he was going to town, he made sure not to wear that green jacket. *–Pat*

Daddy was not a fair-weather friend. And neither was he a flashy friend, i.e. he didn't show off his friendship so the world could give him praise. No, he was a behind-the-scenes friend who helped when folks needed it most but expected it the least, and he did it without expecting (and most of the time, never getting) anything in return.

Some specific examples of this character trait that I personally witnessed are:

- he shared most anything we had with young aspiring, but needy nieces, nephews, and grandchildren

- he secretly gave $1000 to a neighbor whose house had just burned to the ground

- he bought a used car for a sharecropper on our farm whose two sons were in their late teens and "needed" transportation. They agreed to repay him with crop money over the years, but they moved off the farm and never paid him back. He didn't seek retribution.

- he voluntarily harvested the crops of his neighbor (who had lost his farm equipment in a fire) before harvesting his own crops.

- he took food to those in need and when they sat too proud to allow him to bring it in the front door, he took it in their back door and placed it in their kitchen cabinets.

- he drove hundreds of miles to attend a funeral or wedding just to show that family that he cared about them, when really, they may have been mere acquaintances. *–Don*

Daddy was a Methodist Church lay speaker, and when he was to speak, he would pick out hymns to go along with his text. On many of these occasions, he would take his three daughters along to play the piano and sing one or more of those hymns during the service It not only taught us to stand before a group with confidence; but taught us many hymns, many of which I know by heart today. He always taught us to be and do our best; to lead, not just to follow. –*Ronna*

Two dating instances: I had a date with a football player after the game one Friday night. Steven brought me home, and we were sitting in his car talking and saying goodnight when suddenly Daddy appears around the corner of the house with a flashlight which he shown right into the driver's side window. It was as if he thought this car had just been driven up and left in his yard, and he was checking it out. Needless to say, after apologizing, saying goodnight to Steven and exiting his car, that was the last date! Of course, Dad tells that he went out to wrap the water pipe and make sure everything was okay for the freeze called for that night. Well he froze any chance at another date with Steven!

The second date of significance: Lynn and I were working over Christmas and the New Year in Bennettsville. A guy at work kept begging me every night to let him take me home. One night when Lynn and I met to get supper late that afternoon, I told her I had agreed to allow Gene to take me home. I told her to tell Daddy that if I wasn't home in fifteen-twenty minutes after work, to come looking for me. After work, Gene walked me to his car, opened the door for me, and then drove me out to a drive-in restaurant to get a coke. I told him that I only agreed to a ride home, did not want a coke, and to please take me home. He bought the coke, which I immediately dumped out on the ground, and again I asked to be taken home. He did just that. When I arrived home, he walked me to the door. Momma and Lynn asked me if I had seen Daddy and convinced me that he had gone looking for me. I was so embarrassed. I said goodnight to Gene, and he left. After asking what time he left the house and worrying a bit, Daddy appears, and everyone dies in laughter! Of course, this little scenario was concocted by Daddy, and he achieved the results he was looking for. All these years later, I have never stopped feeling bad about the way I treated Gene. But we have all laughed about Daddy's little trick. *–Ronna*

About a year after I entered the Air Force, I was assigned to Pope AFB in Fayetteville, North Carolina, for C-130 training before they sent me to Vietnam. Training included low-level flying, and one of the routes went right over our farm. Just like Dad on his return from the war, I got excited about flying over the house and farm. We told everyone that when I flew over, we would rock the wings back and forth so they would know it was me. What we didn't know at the time was the water tower near Gibson, North Carolina, was a landmark for course adjustments on the route. That meant that every C-130 that flew that route would correct course (rock the wings) right over our farm. That was a joke about how I could be on so many planes at once. There were also problems with this. The eyes of those driving the tractors and plowing the small cotton were watching the planes instead of what they were plowing. In a few seconds, you could destroy a lot of cotton. I am sure Dad was glad when my training ended at Pope. *–Pete*

As each of us went off to college, Daddy did something unheard of, and astounds anyone who is told of it today. He went to Gibson to the bank and told them to honor any check written on his account by that child or children while away from home. Each of us was given a checkbook. We were to pay school bills and expenses with a check designating what each check was for at the bottom. He never told us, but it was understood, we would only write a check for necessary expenses. Brother Pete wrote so many checks for "Miscellaneous" that Dad asked Pete to bring "Miss Cellaneous" home with him; he would like to meet "her"! Pete wasn't the only one to write checks for miscellaneous. We all did. However, none of the five children ever took advantage of a Loving, Trusting Father, ever! Some of those school checks are souvenirs of ours today. They remind us of our father's generosity, love, and trust. –*Ronna*

When we were small, Daddy pulled our baby teeth with pliers. However, to fool us kids, Daddy named those pliers "pullikens". Since I was the youngest, I heard Daddy say time and time again, "go get the pullikens" when each of my siblings' many teeth needed pullin'.

At Clemson, I majored in Agricultural Education, and in my junior year, took an Ag Shop course. As I was thumbing through my textbook, I noticed in a picture various wrenches we'd used on the farm. These were marked with a letter of the alphabet with a corresponding alphabetical listing of names of each wrench below. I looked at wrench (a), identified it mentally and checked the listing to see if I was correct. I got them all correct until I identified the pullikens. The book had them "misidentified" as "needle-nosed pliers". How could that be? There was an obvious typographical error that was made in publishing that textbook!

A few days later, we were in the lab, divided into groups of two to practice welding. We took turns laying a welding bead, chipping off the slag, and critiquing each other's work. During my turn, I laid the bead, raised my mask with the intent to begin chipping the slag off the bead, but the bonded metal was glowing red hot, and I'd need a tool with which to pick it up. I asked my partner, who was just raising his mask, to "Hand me the pullikens," and I motioned to the set laying on the bench to his right. He was very confused and asked, "The what?" His delay in reaching for that tool that was two feet from us frustrated me. I just figured he had little "farm sense". So, I picked 'em up myself! He said, "Oh, you mean the needle-nosed pliers." Obviously, he had become misinformed, probably by that same picture with the typo error in our textbook!

That evening, I pondered his actions, and remembered the picture in the book. I took that book to the professor along with a pair of pullikens and asked the professor to identify them. He said they were needle-nosed pliers and asked why. I don't remember my answer, but I did NOT tell him that a twenty-one-year-old man believed that they were called "pullikens" because his dad had nicknamed them such to fool his children! I also began to wonder if Daddy had named the "tooth fairy" incorrectly! –*Don*

Sitting around the table one day after we were all grown and had families of our own, we were telling Daddy and Mama things they did to us as children that we disliked them for. I said I always hated the lectures we got; that the entire time Daddy was lecturing, I was thinking to myself, "Why doesn't he just spank me and get this over with?" At that point, he looked at me and said: "How old are you now, forty? Is that right? Well, see, if I had spanked you, you would have forgotten it by the next day. You're forty years old, and you've never forgotten those lectures." –*Pat*

Dad taught us to love and care for animals. He rode Black Beauty, a five gaited saddle mare, and taught each of us to enjoy riding her. We also rode mules. We even tried to ride a calf Lynn had won in a contest. Lynn was the only one who succeeded! The rest of us could not stay on. Lynn, with her long legs, wrapped them around the calf's belly and crossed them to lock them, so she wouldn't fall off. She didn't fall off, but she slid around and ended up with her legs on top and her body underneath.

We used the horses and mules to mind cows, work the fields, and then for pleasure. There was hog-killing time, when we were taught how to prepare meat and food. We were taught how to kill and dress a chicken. We were taken to the cannery to store up for the winter all the good vegetables we had grown in the garden. Dad taught us to be thrifty and prepare for bad times. *–Ronna*

Daddy expected the same discipline and respect from the farm animals as from us. When I was about six or seven, we had one Holstein cow named Lib who produced lots of milk but wouldn't let a human touch her without kicking. So, Daddy milked the other cows and tried to get Lib to adopt their calves. But Lib refused to allow any calf other than hers to nurse. One night, Daddy and Lib, each with steel wills, squared off. As soon as Daddy eased the orphan to her side, Lib kicked. Daddy yelled at her, moved the calf in closer, and Lib caught the little fellow on his jaw. Daddy yelled again and leaned heavily on her hipbone so that if she raised her leg to kick, she'd lose her balance and not kick. Great idea that worked on most cows, but not Lib. Daddy became more frustrated until he grabbed a thin cable. She kicked, he hit. This went on for several rounds, until one or two of the whelps he'd inflicted barely cut her skin, exposing tiny blood droplets. I began to cry, and said to Daddy, "That's enough, now." And my words, along with Lib's kicks, only served to increase

Daddy's frustration, and I finally sobbingly shouted, "Daddy, you're hurting her! Now stop it!" In one continuous motion, Daddy moved his left hand from the pressure he put on her hipbone and took the cable from his right hand, grabbed my left arm right under my armpit with his now free right hand and pulled me right up by the calf, while simultaneously saying, "Okay, the next time she kicks, I'll whip you!" As he took the cable in his right hand, and turned to lean against her hip with his left, I thought of what was about to occur, and though I was very young, I drew upon wisdom from some source unknown, and cried out, "Hit her again, Daddy!" I never challenged him about discipline thereafter. *–Don*

Dad always set an example. His character was never questioned. One example that I recall seeing honesty and truthfulness in action was the day Uncle Roy came and gave him a check that was for $300 more than he owed him. I watched as Dad wrote him a check for the amount of overpayment and gave it to him. *–Ronna*

When I was a senior in high school, my brother Pete called from Clemson. He said he had a date for me for the freshmen rat-hop. I was to leave home, go by Winthrop, pick up his date, and on to Clemson. Before leaving home in the black '56 Buick (better known as the tank) whose speedometer didn't work, Daddy gave me some money and a blank check and said: "You are the lightest one in my family and have the heaviest foot. When you get caught for speeding, don't give them your money, write them a check." Well, as luck would have it, on my way back home, I was pulled over for speeding (remember the speedometer did not work) and fined $20.00. Upon arriving home, Mama & Daddy were on the front porch. I said to

Daddy, "Remember that blank check you gave me? Well, I had to use it."

He thought I was kidding. Once I convinced him that I was being truthful, he went into a tirade because I didn't tell the officer that my speedometer was broken. Finally, he said, "Young lady, that is one twenty dollars you will pay me back if it takes you until the day you die." After about twenty-five years, I went up to him and handed him a $20.00 bill. He wanted to know what it was for and I said, "So that I will no longer hear the voice in my head that keeps saying "Young lady. . .until the day you die." Needless to say, he didn't remember ever telling me that, but I felt better knowing my debt was paid. *–Pat*

The sun was shining that morning, but by afternoon just in time for my wedding, the rain came down in torrents. Dad's thoughtfulness was extra special. First, he enlisted my brother Don's help with two umbrellas each to walk me from the back of the church where I dressed to the front porch where I entered, trying to keep me dry! Later in the evening as the reception was drawing to a close, he comes up to me and whispers that I and my new husband could have the "Bridal Suite" upstairs room to ourselves if we would consent to stay at home for the night, since it was still raining and bad outside as well as pitch dark. He said it would make him and Mom real happy, and they would feel much better. We respectfully declined, of course! Chuck and I didn't go far, just to Hartsville, because the weather really was bad. I called home to tell Dad that I had left my overnight case (that looked exactly like my sister Lynn's) and just to be sure that Lynn took hers, and not mine, home with her. Now Dad had another opportunity to make this a memorable night. He persuades Lynn and Al that I am in dire need of this overnight case and that they should bring it to me. Therefore, an hour or so later, unexpected by Chuck and me, Lynn and Al show up at the hotel on my wedding night with the case, knocking on the door! Of course, there is much more to this story, but we won't tell it here. Leave it to good ole Dad! –*Ronna*

The summers of my high school years, Daddy had me grading tobacco in the pack-house. After school started my senior year, I did not want to grade the last of the tobacco, and most of it subsequently molded in the pack house, causing it to be of little or no value.

When it came time for McColl High's homecoming, I was asked to be a homecoming queen candidate. Mama and I went shopping. Mama bought me a beige suit to wear in the homecoming parade and a brown suit to wear to the big game. While looking for matching shoes, I found a pair of spiked-heeled lizard skin shoes, but Mama would not pay the $24.95 price to buy them without my asking Daddy's permission.

When I asked Daddy for the shoes, he responded, "Do you think you can buy them with the money made on the molded tobacco in the pack-house?" There was no further discussion because I had just been told, in so many words, that because I had not graded the tobacco, it had molded, and was worth nothing.

Later that night, as I lay in bed crying, Daddy came in. "Have you ever known either of your sisters to need anything that they didn't get?" "No, Sir," I answered. "Have you ever known either of your sisters to want for much that they didn't get?" "No, Sir." "Well, you can get the shoes, BUT they will be the shoes you homecoming in, the shoes you graduate high school in, the shoes you go to college in, the shoes you graduate college in, and the shoes you get married in because I ain't ever going to buy another pair!"

Eight years later, I was cleaning out some of my things from home (at Mama's request) and was going to discard old shoes worn in weddings of family and friends. The lizard skin shoes had seen their best days, so they were going out, too. On the way out the door, Daddy inquired as to what I was hauling out. Upon seeing these lizard skin shoes, he said he paid a lot of money for them, and I had better not put them in the garbage. It is now 2006, almost forty-four years later, and I'm still afraid to get rid of them. Each time I think about it, I recall those words of long ago—Daddy says NO! I guess my son will throw them out when I die, because they will still be in my house! —*Pat*

One of my special memories of Dad occurred in early spring and summer. Daddy worked from before sunrise 'till after dark. After supper and dressed in his khaki shorts, "V-necked" T-shirt and barefooted, he would sit down in the old green woven rocker on the porch corner. When ready for bed, I would go to the porch. Daddy would pat his legs for me to come sit, and I would get in his lap. He would hug me tight and rock in the cool night breeze. I'm sure he told me how much he loved me and other conversation, but I don't remember conversation, only that I was in Daddy's lap, snuggled close, and wrapped in his love. Sometimes it was raining, and the smell of the earth was hearty and wonderful. I would soon fall asleep and Daddy would take me to bed. We didn't have a lot of time in minutes and hours with Daddy, but what we had was quality time—we never doubted we were loved. —*Ronna*

I was a rising high school senior, and Daddy said that since we were the first ones on the school bus in the mornings and the last ones off in the afternoon, I might as well be paid to drive the bus. All kids loved it when the bus was late in the mornings, and we were late to school. Well, that never happened on my watch, because if my bus wouldn't start, Daddy would go get the tractor and chain, and pull me up the road until my bus started, so that we wouldn't be late to school. –*Pat*

Daddy had a great sense of humor and loved to tell a story or a joke to make people smile and laugh. He was not easily embarrassed, and while he was crafty and calculating at times, he was also very spontaneous. Sometime during family meals, someone would invariably say, "Pass me a biscuit." Without hesitation, Daddy would reach into the biscuit warmer, grasp one of Momma's homemade ultra-thin biscuits, and sail it like a Frisbee across the table to the requester! And Momma would look a gasp and say, "Jack! You're teaching these children bad manners!" And all of us, Daddy and Momma included, would have a good laugh. –*Don*

Ethell making biscuits

Daddy loved his wife and kids. He told Momma over and over how special she was to him, and he told us in Momma's presence how much she meant to him and to us. "There's never been and never will be another woman like your mother." And he would explain his love for us by asking us if we knew how much he loved us. And we'd say "Yes, sir." (He taught us that a youngster to his elder, especially to Daddy and Momma, ALWAYS responded "Yes, sir" or "Yes, ma'am" to whatever was asked. And he also taught us to address our elders with the respectful titles of Mr. or Miss, i.e. Mr. Lawrence and Miss Julia.) But no sooner had we said "yes, sir" than he followed with, "If we were all trapped in the house by a gunman outside, and one had to die so the others could escape, you know, don't you, that I'd take the bullet for you?" On my graduation night, unbeknownst to me, he proved that point. I had recently started dating a young lady who had broken up with one of my classmates. On previous dates, this fellow had attempted to intimidate me as he followed us from time to time, and actually fired a pistol aimed high and above my car. Daddy asked what was going to happen as we planned to attend the graduation party. I told him I didn't know, but I'd work through it. When I came home early, he asked me why I had driven my car off the dirt road to the cabin where the party was being held, and why I had allowed my date to get out of the car to speak with the spurned beau when he blocked our path to her home. I asked how he knew that those things had happened, and he said, "I followed you to be sure you and your date were going to be safe!" My embarrassment that my father had followed me all night was totally overshadowed by the security he offered by such sacrificial love and concern. He still exhibits it to all his family to this day. –*Don*

The Newton Reunion was always a special occasion. The church would be completely full of people standing everywhere there was a space. There might be another hundred or so on the porch or outside listening through the windows (which were open since there was no air conditioning). Most of our cousins would be there, from first through maybe fourth or fifth cousins, and we would play together most of the day. Tables would be lined up beside the church from near the highway all the way to the back of the church, and simply loaded with the best food imaginable. After I turned fourteen and got my driver's license, we would pile about fourteen or more of us into the 1956 Buick and head to Lake Wallace (a man-made lake which had recently been completed in Bennettsville) shortly after we ate. It was a sight to see with four or more crammed into the front seat, six or more in the back seat, and the rest jammed into the trunk. That would be illegal today, but what fun we had back then. *–Pete*

The grand kids pile in the truck to go swimming

During the summers, we usually had a large pile of watermelons between the two pecan trees to the side of the house. We had enough that Daddy would tell us to "just drop 'em and bust 'em and just eat the heart out of 'em and bust another one if you want some more". We made a game of seeing who could spit the watermelon seeds the longest distance! Often when we had a lot of company, and especially after the Newton Reunions, he would use the watermelons "for supper".

Mama would go to prepare supper for everyone, and Daddy would tell her to hold off. The next thing you knew, Daddy had set up "watermelon benches" in the yard, sliced up as many watermelons as he thought he might need, and called out to everybody, "Come get some watermelon!" This would fill everyone enough that they would be too full to want supper. –Lynn

Daddy was a great provider for us. We didn't have everything we wanted, but we certainly had everything we needed, and most of what we wanted. We thought we were rich materially and didn't know that we weren't. But it was obvious that we seemed better off than many around us. Momma knew how to stretch every dollar. She'd bake a ham for dinner and the next day's lunch. Then, she'd slice it up for sandwiches for the next day's lunch, and then literally pick every minute speck of meat off the bone for a stew and for seasoning vegetables she'd cook later. Then, she'd freeze the meatless hambone, months later seasoning a big pot of dried beans with it. When she threw that bone out, even the dogs hardly wanted it because it was totally used up.

One spring when I was about six years old, I tripped along in Daddy's footsteps (as I always did) as he walked to the barn. Because it was mid-morning but still pretty chilly, Daddy walked to the East side of the barn and sat down on the concrete barrier at the door of one of the mule stables. I nestled up beside him. He was talking to me about hard stuff. . .stuff I couldn't comprehend. He mentioned a bad crop last fall. He mentioned many unpaid bills, and not knowing where the money would come from to get provisions to begin this year's planting. I just sat there, picking up little, tiny pebbles, tossing them at the baby frogs. Finally, Daddy got up and started walking again. I tripped along behind.

Years later, my small daughter asked a question regarding a family tragedy. I didn't know the answer and was just as lost as she was. I began to think out loud as she sat there beside me. Finally, I considered all the issues at hand and made the most logical decision I could. And we made it through that tough time. But as I sat there with her, I was transported back to that spring morning where Daddy was searching for answers. I realized that he didn't know everything. He wasn't all-wise, all-knowing as I had believed him to be. He was from time to time just as lost in problems as we, in our youth, were. But he had to be responsible. He had to face the adversity, analyze it, and with determination, make it happen for good. When I had trouble removing a bolt from the car engine in my teens, Daddy had said, "If I have to pay a mechanic money to remove that bolt, he's gonna have the same trouble you're having, but he's gonna figure a way to get it off. And if he can, so can you. Now go get it off." In my mind, I've heard that scenario and remembered the morning at the barn hundreds of times in my adult life as I've faced adversities, analyzed the issues, and "made it happen" for good to provide for myself and my family. –*Don*

Daddy and Mama were married for fifty-six years before she died in 1996. Daddy told of their fiftieth anniversary celebration. It was such a joy for us to see them enjoy their friends and family and "their day". One of the things I so enjoyed doing (with some help from Ronna and the others) was finding and cutting out pictures from magazines and creating a comical "scrapbook" of sorts about their life together. It was a fun book to do with sort of a "take-off" on how they met, became engaged, married, and had their family. We presented this "50 Years of Remembering" to them, along with the other gifts he mentioned, the night before their celebration. It was another highlight of their fifty years together as they really seemed to enjoy the book and reminiscing about what a wonderful life they had enjoyed and shared, and how God had blessed them and their family. *–Lynn*

Ethell and Jack enjoying the fiftieth anniversary scrapbook

Ethell and Jack enjoying the fiftieth anniversary scrapbook

My family and I arrived at the farm in the wee hours of the morning after Mama had passed away. Daddy had already gone to bed, so I didn't see him until about 7:00 a.m. When he hugged me, he said: "When I knew your Mama was so sick, I asked the Lord to let me live long enough to take care of her. The minute she died; I asked the Lord not to leave me here without her."

I truly believe he did not want to stay on this earth without Mama—that is, until he met Murl, and then I think he must have asked the Lord for many more years. As of January 2006, they have had eight years together. —*Pat*

When Mama was carried to the Medical University in Charleston in January 1996, I guess Daddy thought he would only be there for a day or two, so he only carried one change of clothes. After a couple of days, Libby and I went shopping and bought him 2 or 3 outfits. The next morning, he got up, showered, and dressed. He entered the room where we all were. With a pose to the left, he said, "Don't I look good?". Then a pose to the right and said, "Don't I look great?" Then, shocking all of us, he turned around, bent over, and said, "See my butt!" He had on one of his new outfits and was showing it off, leaving us all in hysterics. *–Pat*

Dad and Mom came to visit Libby and me when we were stationed in Germany. One of the places we took them to, was the remains of the Remagen Bridge. Daddy really didn't want to go, and I don't think Mom thought the idea was good either. We did not know of the horrible memories he had upon return from war, so we thought it would be special. Mom told us later that he had nightmares for about six months after they returned home. My apologies, Dad. *–Pete*

After Mom died, we were sure Dad was in his last days. All of the life left his eyes. Then one time when I was down home, I noticed a small twinkle that had been missing for a while. I couldn't get him to talk about it, but he was definitely "coming back". He began visiting us in Raleigh a bit more than normal. One day when he showed up, he asked to use the phone. That number caught my eye when the bill came, and I made note of it. Any time any of us traveled, he would always have us call to let him and Mom know we had arrived safely. That is what he had done for Murl, not realizing the information he had left for the "Snoop Patrol". Months later when he was looking for her number, I told him if he was looking for Murl's number, that I had it. What surprise came on his face. "What do you know about Murl?" he asked. "Only that you called her from my house according to my bill." *–Pete*

Murl called one night, frantic that a stranger was at her door and describing him somewhat. (I could only imagine it was "devilish" Murl, whom I had never talked to nor met). I told her I did not know who she was or why she called me, but the description did seem vaguely familiar. I told her to lock the door and call the Police, and under no circumstances let him in. She didn't listen, and she'll have to live with that decision the rest of her life. I made up a "Wanted" poster of Dad and sent to her later, which seemed to circulate quite freely around Plymouth for everyone to "enjoy"! *–Pete*

More than any other gift, Dad gave us a safe, comfortable, loving home, by loving and cherishing our mother always and demonstrating that love before us. He taught us respect and generosity of loving, caring, and sharing through example.

Long truck and car rides just to talk. These were times just to discuss some subject one to one when Dad felt the need to offer advice and counsel; to share some truth or show concern; to talk over a problem, or just be together. *–Ronna*

On Sunday before Momma died, with so much family visiting her at MUSC in Charleston, I found Daddy and asked if he had given any thought to where he was in relation to home and his desires should Momma not make it. I entreated him to give me direction should that happen. He disappeared for a long time. After inquiring if anyone had seen him or knew where he went, suddenly he came down the hall in his sock feet with paper and pen in hand. He got me and took me back to an empty room where he had been all that time. He began to read off the list he had made of all the things we needed to do and all the people he wanted us to contact. He went over each "bullet" on the paper and elaborated on each one. He left nothing to chance. He had given much time and thought to every detail. I look back even now and see his strength and fortitude in such worry and grief. His deep love for Mom and his unfailing desire to give her his best, had helped him put in writing his last wishes for her on earth. On that Tuesday when she died and the days that followed, he didn't have to worry or think, he had already made preparation, and we were able to provide what he desired. It was such a blessing. It made everything so much easier.

On that fateful morning, I believe Momma had a heart attack due to arrhythmia. When they stabilized her, they moved her to ICU. Daddy took time to eat the food from Momma's breakfast tray that she had been unable and unwilling to eat; I believe instinctively knowing that it would be a very long day. We got a nurse to take him to ICU where Momma was while Lynn and I got all of his and Momma's belongings together and loaded onto a large moveable cart, knowing if Momma survived she wouldn't come back to that floor, and if she died, we would need to load the car. We then joined Dad. We had said our goodbyes to Momma earlier; when we thought she was dying that morning. She died about 4 p.m. When we were allowed to see her, Daddy stood at the gurney above her head, cupped her face with his hands and said to her he didn't know how he could go home without her, and he certainly didn't know how to leave her there. When we left ICU and Momma, we went back to the floor to get everything to load the car. Dad took the time to thank the nurses and other staff who had taken care of Mom. He was always thinking of others. Lynn and I went to the parking deck and brought our cars to the loading area, agreeing that Dad should ride with her, since she had the bigger, more comfortable car. After saying our goodbyes to all the wonderful folks at MUSC, as Dad stood at

the car door to get in, he said to me, "Who's riding with you?"
I said, "The Lord; I won't be alone." I led us out of Charleston,
and just before the Florence exit, we stopped to get gas; she at
the outside pump furthest from the station and I at the pump
close to the station. I was preparing to pay, when I looked
up and see Dad coming toward me and asking if I picked up
strangers or would let a stranger ride with me. I told him it
depended on the stranger; if it was him, I would be happy to
have the company. He insisted on paying for the gas, then got
in and rode with me the rest of the way home. We talked all
the way about Mom, their wishes, the plans for the funeral,
etc. When we arrived in Bennettsville, he wanted to stop at
Whitner-Evans Funeral Home and explain to Mr. Evans why
we weren't using his services for Mom's funeral. Again, he
was thinking of others even in his grief.

In the weeks and months that followed, I came home every weekend after work to take care of Dad, arriving home
on Friday evening. Dad would meet me at the door crying.
We talked into the night and all day on Saturday. He relived
his memories of Momma and their years together, of the war,
of his childhood, of friends and neighbors and how kind and
caring they had all been. We would be laughing one minute
and crying the next. I heard stories I had heard many times in
my lifetime, and some I didn't remember ever hearing before.
I would pick up and straighten the house, cook our meals, and
prepare food to be left for him to eat during the week. He
would tell me where important papers were and what to do
if he died. He was forever worrying about his children and
not wanting to be a burden on any of us. When I left on Sunday afternoon, we were both crying. I did this for over a year.
Then one Friday I came home, and Dad wasn't crying, and after some conversation he was actually smiling and confessing

his dates with a lovely lady. He eventually married Murl, and what a change she made in his life. I got to know my Daddy, really know my Daddy, during those weekends. I felt so honored and privileged that I could give back to him and do small things for him during his time of need, but as always Daddy gave me so much more. That time with Daddy was priceless, and I wouldn't trade it for the world.

Thank you, Daddy. *–Ronna*

There seems to be no end to the memories of you, Dad. My list goes on and on. You've done and been so much, time and space don't allow for it all. However, I cherish and treasure every moment, every picture, and every wonderful memory! You are a lover of Liberty, uncompromising on principles, truthful, honest, a lover of your children, compassionate, a doer, a servant of servants–truly no ordinary man. You're superior! You're like a tree–a fixed person; stable, steadfast, unmovable. You're a growing individual–though the outward part weakens, the inward part is renewed and gets stronger day by day. You are fruitful of golden deeds. You are a beautiful, living creature–you retain your attractiveness, for how beautiful is a good life! Psalm 1:3. You have always done what you must. You gird yourself with determination and fight your daily battles out of true convictions, never failing love, and undying loyalty. You keep an unfaltering trust that God will see you through. "He alone is great, who by a life heroic conquers fate."

The demands upon a father are great. Our world demanded courageous minds, watchful eyes, ready hands, true faith–actually many hearts in one–and God answered the call by giving the world fathers. The qualities of his heart seem to be a thousand hearts and each heart an absolute necessity to fatherhood. This makes him An Ideal.

I wish I were as big a man,

as big a man,

as bright a man,

I wish I were as right a man in all this earthly show,

As broad and high and long a man,

As strong a man, as fine a man, As pretty near divine a man
   as one I used to know.

I wish I were as grave a man,

As brave a man,

As keen a man,

As learned and serene a man, as fair to friend and foe;

I wish I owned sagaciousness

And graciousness, As should a man Who hopes to be as
   good a man as one I used to know.

I'd be a creature glorious,

Victorious,

A wonder-man,

Not just-as-now a blunder man whose ways

And thoughts are slow,

If I could only be the man,

One-half of one degree the man,

I used to think my father was, when I was ten or so.

That poem was written by Benton Braley.

May I add that you are every bit that man, the Father I now do know!

We esteem you Dad because of your heroism. Your sweat and tears and blood, shed for us, testify to your heroic nature. He who struggles for others when the easy way is to run, is a hero, call him what you will. We know the brave story of your sacrifices, rigorous toil, long hours, many jobs, unremitting thrift, the slow accumulation of savings, at time bitter discouragement, but also the outpouring of happiness as you realized your hopes for your children. I hope we have made you proud and reached at least some of your dreams for each of us.

Too often we forget the price you've paid. We enjoy the fruits of your labors but fail to see the labors themselves. The world sees the glitter of the gold and not the sweat of your sacrifices.

Perhaps we have been woefully negligent in honoring you our heroic Dad, who takes the wounds of the everyday struggles of life. We are protected because you courageously dared. The highest and noblest spirit is "that a man lay down his life for another". Dad you did this not in one supreme gift, but in the giving of yourself little by little, day by day. The daily conflicts of earning a living and heading a household brought out the slumbering qualities of and revealed my hero.

I say to you, my dearest Daddy; your unselfish, glorious deeds shall never die. They shall ever be hallowed in the cherished memory of a grateful daughter and her children, and theirs for generations to come!

I love you so very much. I regret I haven't been more and done more to show you just how much. You are truly my "Daddy" and I love you. May every day be your day, special in every way. And may you know every day in every way that my love and prayers are with and for you.

Thanks for the Memories. Thanks for all you've been and done. I will always be eternally grateful to my Heavenly Father, for giving me my earthly Father and Mother who helped to mirror on earth a Heavenly Father's love.

–*Your second oldest daughter, Ronna*

I read in an Ann Landers newspaper column an article from a daughter who was given a piece of paper to fill with anything she chose to go into a "scrapbook of memories" for her parent's sixtieth anniversary. She asked her parents (on her paper) how she could say "Thank You", or repay them, or what she could give them for all they had done for her over the years. How could she measure the worth of their love, and what gift would be enough? When the answer came to her, it was to give and to be to her own children what her parents had given and been to her. The final paragraph on her paper read: "And someday, maybe, they will come to me and say, 'How can we thank you for all you have done for us?' And I will tell them, 'Don't thank me. Thank my parents. For I am the product of their love, and you are my greatest gift to them.'"

Thank you, Daddy, for what you and Mama have given me. I am so eternally appreciative of your love and sacrifices. I love you both so much, and my husband and children love you and admire you; and I hope that I, and they, have grown to be somewhat as you had hoped, and desired, and prayed for. I love you, Daddy.

And I thank you from the bottom of my heart.

–*Your oldest daughter, Lynn*

The song "Daddy's Hands" was written and recorded by Holly Dunn in loving memory of her father. Over the years, every time I hear this song, I sing along, knowing that it describes our Dad in every way. It tells of calloused hands, praying hands, hands that had seen years of work and worry, loving hands, supporting hands, hands soft and kind yet hard as steel–not always gentle–but always loving. If you want to really know my daddy, find this song and listen to it. *–Your youngest daughter, Pat*

My Lovely Lady
> She's looking down from above,
> Sending each of us her love.
> We know where she is, you see.
> There's where she wants each of us to be.
> If in Jesus, we put our trust
> God's grace is surely sufficient for us.
> Live for Him daily and you will be Heaven bound – up here
> with me.
> Then worry not about your past.
> Jesus' love and salvation will forever last.
> Then live for the future and eternity.
> A child of God – This you will forever be.
> I join with her in wishing each of you a Christ-filled Christ-
> mas And a Blessed New Year.
> *PJN, Composed by Peter Jack Newton*
> Thanksgiving, 1996

PETER JACK NEWTON

EPILOGUE

With "Thanks" to My Heavenly Father, and with all of His many, many blessings, I celebrated my ninetieth birthday on Saturday, July 8th, 2006. My immediate family—my wonderful wife Murl, along with my five wonderful children—surprised me with quite a celebration for the event. It was at the community center at Boykin Church which was decorated with a large flower arrangement, a "Money Tree" of ninety $1.00 bills, and over 100 bright, colorful balloons, all thanks to daughter Ronna and her family. There were also several large ninetieth birthday posters and a slide presentation from my birth to present supplied by son Don; and a beautiful three-tiered birthday cake with a large candy "90" on top, made and decorated by daughter Lynn. Murl had the event catered, and a delicious meal was enjoyed by all. Most all of my family, as well as most of Murl's—children, grandchildren, great-grandchildren, step-grandchildren, step-great-grandchildren, and others were present. What a surprise! What an event! What a day of honor! What a loving family I do have!

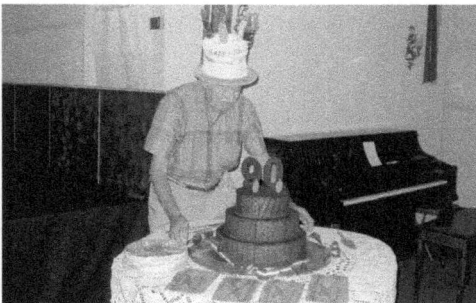

Jack's 90th birthday celebration

And what a devoted Church Family and friends I have also! After Saturday's excitement, the members of Boykin United Methodist Church "surprised" and "honored" me again on Sunday, July 9th, proclaiming it "Peter Jack Newton Day". I had been told there was to be a covered dish dinner at the church. This was nothing new—Boykin folks love to eat, and quite often! Some of the children had stayed overnight and were to join us for church and dinner. What a surprise when we arrived for church! There were all the Boykin people, the children, friends from Plymouth, hunting buddies, etc., etc.! What a crowd! Some of my favorite hymns were used in my honor within the worship service. I was presented with a plaque from the church and lots of greetings, comments, and stories from family and friends. In the church bulletin was a poem written just for me, and a number of pictures depicting various events in my life. The first printing of this book was presented and "sold out" at the "covered-dish" dinner and social festivities enjoyed at the community center.

Jack and Murl – Honored by Boykin Church on his 90th birthday

The honor and love are awesome! God has blessed me–Oh! So much! I thank Him! And I thank you–all of you–who have ever, in any way, been a part of my life.

PJN
July, 2006